Innovisions

EXPRESSIONS OF CREATIVITY IN DANCE

By the same author:
Creativity in Dance

Innovisions

EXPRESSIONS OF CREATIVITY IN DANCE

Coralie Hinkley

The utilization of expressive, imaginative, creative elements within the mesh of ideas, insights, movement, realised into choreographies and compositions. The source and substance of these creative experiences are a means of creating in dance as a performing art and in dance education.

First published in 1990
by Cygnet Books

Distributed by University of Western Australia Press
Nedlands, W.A. 6009

Agents: Eastern States of Australia, New Zealand and Papua New Guinea: Melbourne University Press, Carlton South, Vic. 3053; U.K., Europe, Africa and Middle East: Peter Moore, P.O. Box 66, 200a Perne Road, Cambridge CB1 3PD, England; U.S.A., Canada and the Caribbean: International Specialized Book Services Inc., 5602 N.E. Hassalo Street, Portland, Oregon 97213, U.S.A.; Singapore and Malaysia: National University of Singapore Multi-Purpose Co-operative Society Ltd, Ground Floor, Central Library, Kent Ridge, Singapore 0511.

National Library of Australia
Cataloguing-in-Publication data

Hinkley, Coralie.
  Innovisions, expressions of creativity in dance.

  Bibliography.
  ISBN 0 85564 309 9.

  1. Modern dance — Philosophy. 2. Creation (Literary, artistic, etc.). I. Title.

792.8

Designed and phototypeset by University of Western Australia Press, Nedlands, Western Australia.
Printed and bound by Silex Enterprise & Printing Co., Hong Kong.

"It would seem that dancing came into being at the beginning of all things, and was brought to light together with Eros, that ancient one, for we see this primeval dancing clearly set forth in the choral dance of the constellations and in the planets and fixed stars, their interweaving and interchange and orderly harmony."[1]

[1] *The Dance of Shiva.* Ananda K. Coomaraswamy. The Noonday Press, 1957, U.S.A. The formation of the world and the birth of the gods, Eros or Cupid; Uranus Group or the Sky crowned with stars.

Contents

Author's Note

Over the years I have kept notebooks, essays, photographs, questions on aspects of dance, insights by creative artist-teachers, many of whom have had considerable influence in shaping my development and outlook as a dancer, choreographer, creative teacher, in the art form of the modern or contemporary dance. At best these notebooks are a record to register fragments of the deeply rooted aspects of that involvement. Now they may serve with memory to reveal and clarify glimpses of those dance experiences which form my background.

So to understand the present one has to know the past . . . to express in words that which has been realised in movement.

> the past, in fact, is never really discarded only expanded, encompassed and eventually transcended . . .[1]

My aim then is to share aspects of these influences and impressions selected from the flow of dance material which I believe has increased my awareness to free "the peculiar power of seeing with the mind, which is the imagination"[2] and to describe the outcomes of my experiences within the nature of creativity, through ideas, thoughts and movements drawn from choreography and composition in different situations.

I hope this reflects the faith that I have in common with many human beings that creative freedoms—expressions, initiatives and experiences—be made available to all; not the least important being through the dance . . . a prime area of human expression.

Coralie Hinkley

---

[1] *Arts and Ideas* by William Fleming. Holt, Rinehart and Winston, U.S.A., 1980.
[2] *The Dramatic Imagination* by Robert Edmond. Jones Theatre Art Books, New York, 1980.

Acknowledgments

To the artist-teachers, dancer-performers, dance students and children; to the composers, writers, poets and photographers who inspired me and collaborated with me in the experiences in dance which form part of *Innovisions*.

These associations have given me a deep and lasting knowledge, an enrichment of spirit and the means for the creative impetus in this work.

My warmest thanks to Martha Hill of The Juilliard School of Dance; Helen McGehee and Bertram Ross of The Martha Graham School of Contemporary Dance; Kai Tai Chan of The One Extra Dance Company; Gerard Sibbritt; Bill Pepper; Shona Dunlop MacTavish, for introducing stimulating aspects of dance and drama which were advantageous, to my perspective; The Ririe-Woodbury Dance Company of Salt Lake City, for permission to use the title "Innovisions"; Evelyn Rowe for opportunity in dance at Fort Street Girls' High School; Denise Fletcher for sustained and patient help and careful reading of the manuscript; Mrs B. J. Perry for co-operation and effort in typing the manuscript; John and Vera Hinkley for their gifts to me, which turned into a lifelong love of dance.

Foreword

Creativity in all its phases, forms and stages is man's greatest marvel. In touching upon this miraculous gift I am disposed to say that it is a spark filched from the Creator, bestowing upon this man powers denied the many and instilling in him the consciousness of being apart. Many have tried to define and explain the most awe-inspiring but also puzzling phenomenon of the genius or major talent. But how can one define "otherness", how can one analyze the reasons and motivations for its manifestations?

No doubt talent is basic to genius, but talent may come close to genius without ever reaching it. Any creatively gifted person possesses talent, but the genius is possessed by talent. Even great creative minds repeat, embellish, and extend what has been dealt with before them. The genius creates because he cannot help doing it (Beethoven: "It must be!"); he goes new ways, he often dares without being afraid of finding himself alone. Genius is master of man. Henri-Frédéric Amiel wrote in his Journal: "Doing easily what others find difficult is talent; doing what is impossible for talent is genius."

Man is well aware of the fact that some of his contemporaries have written their names into history; but history will deal with them in its own unpredictable manner, will let their signatures pale, or magnify their imprint. It is surprising how quickly a cultural climate may change and, with it, the significance of the intellectual and artistic heroes of the past; how the taste of time can bypass or even have contempt for men of stature or ignore periods of the past. In the seesaw of historic events, of coming phases and passing fads, even incontestable geniuses sometimes suffer, they may be blacklisted by aesthetes and snobs; but in time they all pretty well weather the ironies of man's changing moods. Creative men are the one constant in the inconstances of life, even though "some are born posthumously", as Nietzsche said.

It will come as no surprise that creative minds have a stunning intellectual capacity which, by its nature, creates a curiosity about all the phenomena of life which is never satisfied. One of the most striking characteristics of the creative person is his readiness for and openness to unlimited experiences. He may be interested in the most insignificant manifestations, but when you see him speak to his shoemaker he will observe and absorb impressions different from those of any average person. The quality and degree of intelligence and intuition play a tricky game. As there are visual and aural types, there are also artists whose intuitive feelings may outweigh their intelligence. In other words, they work at their craft with different stimulations, tools and means. But it seems essential for the artist to have the capacity to record and to retain impressions, experiences and facts, but also the ability to have them available at a creative moment's notice. What distinguishes the intellectual person—who is endowed with the same above-mentioned qualities—from the creative artist, is the latter's ability to form fluently new combinations of all these elements and to formulate them in a new, unusual way, or to channel them into artistic visualizations.

Our wish images play their part in the process of creativity, as all the achievements of civilization seem to come from the taming of the *id*, the reservoir of man's intellectual drives. Freud spoke of philosophers, writers and artists as "the few to whom it is vouchsafed ... with hardly any effort to salvage from the whirlpool of their emotions the deepest truth to which we others have to force our way, ceaselessly groping among torturing uncertainties". The artist's *id* communicates to the ego, and then the same intra-psychic processes are submitted to others. What is important is the ability and power with which the artist can control neuroticism. He shapes his fantasies and gives them social reference. But it has been proved that art and neuroses are not necessarily synonymous, even though the artist's personal conflicts are intimately interwoven in his creations and determine the direction of his artistic development as much as they colour each work. There is an old saying that the artist doesn't see things as they are, but as he is. Cesare Pavese circumscribes this idea when he says that the creatively gifted person achieves complete possession of his own experiences, body, rhythm, and memories. No doubt the creative person gives *Gestalt* to the visions of his mind and imagination: not only because he cannot help doing it, but also because of his conviction that whatever he does is worth doing for the moment that is, for the very day he can create.

More often than not products of highly creative men carry the stamp of the unusual with them, and they are sometimes frightening to the ordinary eye. There can be an intense but disciplined exuberance of spirit and flesh in the creative process that appears completely undisciplined to the person unblessed with such madness. It is difficult to say what is normal, if we don't mean dull, but it is certain that the highly gifted and creative person is a man inspired. And inspiration was defined by Plato as "the divine release from the ordinary ways of man" and as a state of "creative madness". Seneca echoed Plato when he said, "There is no great genius without a touch of madness". The extraordinary height where he exists (and the range of the creatively gifted person is of unlimited scope) inspires his views, gives him the capacity for the unusual, for discovery and creative imaginations. Many of these artists are endowed with an almost seismographic sensibility, their inventiveness may sometimes have a touch of clairvoyance.

The miracle of the creative act can be investigated, researched, and interpreted, but the findings are like sand running through one's fingers. Only if we discover the psychological key to man's creative power, shall we ever learn its secret. Then perhaps we are right when we say that to explain the artistic process psychologically is a contradiction in itself, for the spirit rises out of the *Gestalt*: it is the measure of all being.

If we accept the need of the creative person to express himself and an urgency about doing it, we must have a look at the phenomenon called inspiration without which creativity can hardly exist. Inspiration can reach us in and through different ways. For the choreographer the fascination with music must play a decisive part whereby images and/or dramatic events created through movement are inspired by sound effects on the choreographer's nervous system. There are quite a few literary sources of inspiration—I would call them prefabricated which are a part of our mental existence, such as the Bible, mythology, or Shakespeare, the world of fairytales or legends. One could also speak of "time-conditioned" inspiration. Did not the turn of the century ask for or challenge Isadora Duncan who stood in front of the mirror searching for the soul of the dance which she thought to find in the solar plexus? Was it mere coincidence that her contemporary, Sigmund Freud, tried to discover the mechanism of the human soul? Or could Théophile Gautier have created "Giselle" without having fallen in love with Carlotta Grisi? Certainly, love, the interrelation between human beings is as important a source of inspiration as are our reactions stimulated by historic or contemporary events.

It still remains an inexplicable phenomenon what can work as inspiration, how and at which point it may begin to work on the artist. In the last analysis, it is a spark filched from the Creator leading to an artistic statement for which the artist may be tortured by his critical pangs of conscience, for which he may be judged by his contemporaries and honoured or damned by posterity.

The dance—so often referred to as the mother of the arts—has always had innumerable practitioners but has brought forth only a very limited number of creative talents, i.e. choreographers, who write the scenario and, so to speak, direct it. With the exception of the protean genius of Jean Cocteau, who also tried his hand at choreography, I know of no choreographer who would not have been a dancer first. The physical immediacy and the body as sole instrument of this art necessitate a thorough knowledge of what the body can do. In retrospect it seems that many of the great choreographers have been minor talents as dancers, particularly in the ballet. However, I am inclined to think that, more often than not, these artists gave up dancing as soon as they discovered their choreographic gift.

Most dancer-choreographers of stature have been renowned teachers and a good many of them have been articulate in bringing to paper their thoughts and convictions on their art, as the writer of this book, Coralie Hinkley, proves.

The rebellious artists around the turn of the century, and those who immediately followed them, showed great propensity for articulating their ecstatic feelings in more than one way. The dancers were no exception. In general, the modern dancer in his bare feet and with an open, expressive mind has been more easily articulate than the tradition-bound ballet dancer. Many of these dancers have discharged themselves well as speakers and writers, some of them have shown a natural talent for drawing and painting—as Vaslav Nijinsky developed in his hours of agony in which light and darkness fought within him. Isadora Duncan, the first rebel in the days of the *fin de siècle*, possessed a thoroughly poetic nature with an innate feeling for music, movement, and the word. For Isadora's compatriot and contemporary, Ruth St Denis, who fell in love with the mysticism of the Orient, dancing was a means to a much more important end. Feeling that our civilization was growing decadent because "too many of us take from without instead of giving from within", she became a crusader for the sacred dance. She was an eloquent spokeswoman for her ideas and put some of them down as poems.

There have been many more dancers and choreographers in this century who have given us some volumes of interest. Ted Shawn, Serge Lifar, Pearl Primus and Doris Humphrey wrote about dance and dancers with more than average skill. It is amazing that when dancers turn to writing, their most prosaic topics often show the touch of the poet, as if being a dancer presupposes innate lyricism. Mary Wigman wrote probably the most poetically valid book: *The Language of Dance*.

If a teacher is not a creative teacher he is a bad teacher. His greatest task is to make his student love that with which he is not yet familiar. He must find out that it is easier to reach the student's head if he takes a detour via his heart, since mind and motion are inseparable. How can I light up the spirit if I don't ignite a spark in his emotions?

A student once wrote me that I had changed her life by making a dancer out of her. Of course, I did not do anything of the sort. "We cannot make other people responsible for how we shape our life. You always wanted to become a dancer. I opened your eyes and, at the same time, made you see the beauties and risks involved." A teacher's task can be compared with the work of a plastic surgeon who achieves miracles when he beautifies the face of his patient without changing the expression of his personality.

It is often said the dancer shows no particular inclinations for anything else but the dance, since his natural interest lies in observing how his body moves. I found the contrary more correct, especially among the choreographers and the modern dancers. They are conscious of the fact that their body moves best if their mental eye penetrates their mirror image and if their spirit remains as mobile as their muscles and joints.

When I worked with Ruth St Denis, she had passed her 80th year. Nevertheless, she insisted on making plans for the next 20 years. She taught me to attune my time to the necessities of life and to intimidate death by ignoring him (she was about 96 when she died). Mary Wigman taught me human and artistic integrity. José Limón taught me how to create and express myself with dinity and George Balanchine taught me to doubt each word with which I thought to express myself best. I taught myself to approach each creative work and each word I wrote with humility. For many decades I have worked as a teacher in order to learn something.

The sources and reasons for human creativity and its inspiration will probably have to remain among one of the few enigmas in life with which we should be able to live happily ever after. Art is but revealed by its mysteries. The artist can do little more than trust and truthfully work on himself and his material. After the conclusion of each work one may naturally wonder about who and what gave it the shape it has. But the artist should not give too much of his precious time to the thought of how such achievement was possible. One should accept inspiration as a way to creativity and as something that we encounter on our road to self-fulfilment. One should leave it to the chance of destiny to decide what has come of it. Nietzche thought a great deal about inspiration and came to the conclusion: "One takes and absorbs it without questioning who gave it to us." The philosopher Martin Buber added: "Well, one may not question it, but one should at least say thanks for it."

Professor Walter Sorell,
Dance Critic, Writer, Poet,
New York, Zurich, 1988.

On Creativity

Creation is ourselves; our individual thoughts, acts, gestures, beliefs, leading to shaping the gift that one might possess.

It is a way of seeing, of expanding the sense of reality of one's experiences, sensations, facts, impressions and memories which have been recorded within; re-formed in a new and unusual way, ready to be available at a moment's notice. The conception then can be based on how we feel about ourselves, how we "see" life; utilizing and re-arranging the creative elements by paying attention to our imaginative life; to the fleeting images which give quality to the idea. It is a way of making the spaces so that the insight and rare flash of inspiration can function and flow through the creative processes, with the idea and its development into physical action visualized into dance . . . into choreography.

The creative forces within the individual's sub-conscious life are mysterious, elusive. Those who create do so from an inner necessity; a creative purpose; a passionate intensity.

The experiences of life, the different states of mind and feeling, may cause a transformation in the creative mind, which can become an impulse for creativity and find an outlet in the working process of the art form.

According to Stephen Spender "there is nothing that we imagine that we do not already know . . . to remember what we have already experienced and to apply it to some different situations . . . from beyond our past, beyond ourselves . . . to other lives, other situations, other experiences".[1]

By listening to these obscure fragments of experiences that are hidden from view, yet alive and fluctuating between the inner vision and the external world of reality, we can reveal and develop them and give them a form and meaning.

In creativity the risk is the only path to discovery.

One engages in the process of drawing out of oneself and others through exercising the creative imagination and will, the gift of creativity which Martha Graham says "belongs to all of us, for the instant and if not fostered, dies" . . . one needs to listen and respond to those creative impulses and energies which sustain the ideas as we search to discover the creative language and resolve its development.

In an instant the memory of movement re-kindles within us and the physical, intellectual, imaginative and spiritual elements in the living, breathing, miraculous

[1] *Stephen Spender—The Creative process*, edited by Brewster Ghiselin. A Mentor Book, New York, 1955.

1

human body becomes the means of action for the expression and communication of the creative in dance.

One is called upon to be fluent in the expression of the content; to develop awareness of the implications and possibilities of the essential elements of the idea. It is important that one's concentration be deep enough to reach the level of creating; to free the sensitive decisions of choice, selection, change in the discovery of the movement, space and relationships, extending the understanding of what feeling and meaning may be contained in the conception. To think imaginatively about the dancers; to be concerned about their movement potential, expressive qualities, inner feeling and personality.

The creation takes place between you, the choreographer and the dancer—the relationship of the living movement, the body design, the expression in the space.

Above all, one must maintain the purpose.

It is important to give the opportunity to create, to potential choreographers, creative teachers, creative dancers; to discover a means of expression for themselves by giving it a form in whatever manner they choose. This gift will not develop on its own, requiring scope for development, incentive and recognition; the creative abilities need early detection.

The preliminary efforts by students in making a dance are mostly by trial and error. By availing themselves of the principles of composition by an experienced choreographer or the sensitive perception of a creative teacher, the young dancer can attain and develop the skills to organize the idea. This discipline will lead to further creating; some of it spontaneous; to question; to experiment; a conscious discovery of their own creative process.

The myriad movements of the creative mind in man's fleeting world may be caught between the agitation of leaves and the sighing of waves. The one who loves dance is prepared to enter its mysteries and actualities.

> Superb in its attraction and swift to retreat a thing waiting but for the approach of the right men ... prepared to soar with them through all the circles beyond the earth ... movement.[1]

---

[1] *Gordon Craig—Movement and Dance*, edited and with an introduction by Arnold Rood. Dance Books, London, 1977.

Modern Dance Heritage, Background, Artist-Teachers, Influences

GERTRUD BODENWIESER

I became completely absorbed in the point of view of the modern dance responding passionately to the vision of dance, philosophy, principles and language of movement expressed by Gertrud Bodenwieser,[1]

> we do not ask of our generation to express themselves in the way of those of past generations . . .
> The idea of the new dance is that it has taken up relationship with the great stream of modern living, choosing its topics not only from a fancy world of lightness and charm . . . but a world full of problems and strife, great ideas and development; the modern dance does not wish to be only amusing and entertaining; it aims to be stirring, exciting, and thought provoking. That is the ideal of any real art.[2]

It was a never-ending source to me of wonder, of beauty, both visual and spiritual.

As a dancer being part of the artistic experience of her choreographic works, meant also growth and development of one's musical sensitivities. These were awakened and guided by Dory Stern,[3] who gave us musical security, preserving the interaction between music and the dance; the harmony, power and fluidity for the expression of the dance, dancer and choreographer. This relationship to music was further extended as imaginative accompaniment in dance improvisation or the special interest in a music composition written for a choreographic idea. The hard work, discipline, sacrifice were unimportant to me; only the responses to the inspiration of Bodenwieser's imagination, her artistic concepts, interpretations and dance forms mattered. Thus I emerged as a dancer in the Bodenwieser style, a member of her company and a teacher in her school.

[1] Beginning of dance studies with Gertrud Bodenwieser in Sydney, 1942.
[2] Excerpts Dance programme, Gertrud Bodenwieser, 1940. Sydney Gertrud Bodenwieser—former Professor of Dance and Choreography at Academy of Music and Theatre Arts, Vienna 1924–38. With her European dance company of Viennese dancers, she began her Australian dance period, 1939–59; the foremost pioneer of modern dance in this country, replacing her original group with Australian dancers. Her career as a famed dancer, choreographer, teacher and producer in Vienna ended with the occupation of Austria by Hitler and the Nazis; overcoming strenuous difficulties she made her new dance centre in Sydney.
[3] Dory Stern, pianist, accompanist, associate artist with Gertrud Bodenwieser in Australia, for her school and company, 1941–1956—approximately.

3

The Wheel of Life, Eileen Cramer, Mardi Watchorn, Coralie Hinkley
Choreography: Gertrud Bodenwieser
Photograph: Margaret Michaelis
Background: Gertrud Bodenwieser

The classes provided an insight into ways to transpose movement; different gradations of flow, dynamics, rhythms, expressions; one could elaborate on the original design, transforming it into different qualities and shapes. "Every movement a design in space—the basis of which was the circle."[1] This fluency of the changes that we made to movement was an integral part of Gertrud Bodenwieser's teaching and a method of developing creativeness in her dancers and students; it was for me, *the first stirrings of awareness of creativity*.

We assimilated Bodenwieser's approach to choreography; the intuitive feeling for composition, the insights into "the predicament of man—his joys and sorrows"; opportunity was given to us to create movements within the conception of the subject matter or theme. Fragments of our imagination were threaded through some of the choreographies. For instance in the Life of the Insects, the dancers as beetles experimented with strange and weird articulations of the limbs, as they moved from place to place, pushing and hoarding possessions; sharp runs, uneasy pattern changes expressed the aggressive instincts of ants. The dancers flowed through their organic shapes in the cycle of birth, death, re-birth, within the frame of the inevitability of motion in The Wheel of Life. The experience of the dance imagery in Vision after one of the Etchings of Goya, heightened one's sense of creativity, interpreting Spanish inspired movement in the changing images of good and evil. The beautiful rich young girl fails to recognise the old hag who is following her . . . begging; "Dios La Perdone: Yera Su Madre"; God forgive her—it was her mother!

As dancers our "creative personality"[2] was brought into focus by Gertrud Bodenwieser, who in her search for truth and beauty could touch the human spirit . . . that is why I stayed so long.[3]

THE FIRST STIRRINGS OF CREATIVITY

Unknown Land

Looking back to 1956, and while still with Gertrud Bodenwieser, I composed Unknown Land, a modern dance work portraying a perspective of Australia. I found the imagery in the poetry of Rex Ingamells,[4] leader of the Jindyworobaks; a group of Australian writers in the nineteen forties whose fundamental principle was that Australian culture must be based on the Australian environment. The music for this work was specially written for me by John Antill, Australian composer; first for piano and then for string orchestra. He followed the ideas sensitively, expressing in the composition the feelings of bitter loneliness, anguish and harsh struggle of life in the Australian bush . . . which changed to a mood of energy and hope.

The following extracts refer to the thematic material in relation to the poetry and movement language of the choreography Unknown Land.

THE RED HEART

withdrawn from men, superb, aloof, alone, brooding eternal secrets on her own.

---

[1] Dance Notes, 1943, Gertrud Bodenwieser.
[2] *The New Dance—Gertrud Bodenwieser*, edited by Marie Cuckson. Private edition. Rondo Studios, Sydney, 1970.
[3] 1941 to 1954; 1954–1957.
[4] *Rex Ingamells, 1913–1955, Selected Poems*. Georgian House, Melbourne, 1944.

The space was opened up by wide circular patterns of movement—of broad abstractions; the movement had to fill the space and time; the feeling of parched tracks, the harshness of the desert landscape; the fierce beauty of spirit.

FROM A DYING PEOPLE

I caught the echo of faint cooee crying;
I glimpsed a vision of a people dying.

As if crouching over a dying fire I became the figure of the Aborigine—the space diminished . . . the body reaching into the earth, bruised by the haunting cries at his extermination.

WOMAN OF THE OUTBACK

Through arduous days they shaped a dream-made world To their strong purposes.

The woman of the outback constructed an imaginary house—a dwelling in the vast landscape that would give her security and an identity; she divided the space into geometrical dimensions, travelling the earth with strong realism; pushed, pulled, measured, lifted, thrusted, hammered—manually building her dream with the body . . . until the back-breaking effort dissolved and filled the space with the dance of the last section of Unknown Land.

RIVERINA CELEBRATION

My heart would give you joy of this
that riots in the air,
The vibrant colour, warmth and sound,
Australia everywhere.

NEW EXPERIENCES IN CONTEMPORARY DANCE: NEW YORK

MARTHA GRAHAM

In 1957 I became the first Australian dancer to be awarded a Fulbright Scholarship for the graduate study of modern dance in New York. Discontinuing the pattern of my life and dance in Sydney I went to the United States of America to experience a new rigour of dance, a new reality, a new inspiration with artists whose concepts were changing the face of the contemporary dance.

Through this new experience of dance I came to realise the meaning of the deep psychoanalytical approach of Martha Graham . . . man and his conflict; or

the arc between two deaths

the fall and recovery principle of the technique of Doris Humphrey; the concern with the conflict of man and his environment; or the unpredictability of the structure of dance by Merce Cunningham based on the philosophy of I Ching. They made their statement "the affirmation of life through movement"—it was their truth; they proclaimed their art along with Edward Weston, Paul Klee, Arnold Schoenberg, Frank Lloyd Wright, John Cage.

Coralie Hinkley in the contemporary dance class conducted by Martha Graham
Photograph: Serge Silbey

I confronted this new medium of modern dance and the wisdom of the philosophy and technique of Martha Graham[1] in which "movement never lies; when you move you stand revealed for what you are". This awareness of movement and its articulation through the body, when all excesses were stripped away, became a living, moving sculpture to be shaped, re-shaped, hollowed out, with a pristine quality of its own. The essence of the movement and images were disarmingly simple before developing into a profound and complex definition and form; this original movement language of communication allowed the dancer to mature as an artist through the technique and personality. The daily demands of the physical work sensitizing the nerves, heightening awareness for dramatization, the resonance, purity and deep meaning of which was felt long after the daily "ritual for dance".

LOUIS HORST

I wanted to understand more fully the principles of this new definition of dance. Like many other artists, these second generation modern dancers went *back to the*

[1] The Martha Graham School of Contemporary Dance, New York. (Dance Scholarship.)

Emergence, Group Forms. Composition: Louis Horst.
Dawn Mitchell-Tress, Peggy Brightman (Erlandson), Emily Waddhams
Photograph: Serge A. Silbey

beginning in art and music; to the Greek and Etruscan periods of archaic art, in which they discovered a concern with the formalisations of movement, a planal consciousness in the slow, well co-ordinated gymnopedies of the Pyrrhic dances. These elements could be adapted and related to the modern dance and so create an awakening of a new feeling for dance, alertness, clarity; a new vigour, always moving, a sense of life, as well as a new relationship between music and dance.

Encouraged by the faculty of the Martha Graham School I began studying Pre-Classic and Modern Forms of dance composition directed by composer Louis Horst.[1] The concepts intensified my perceptions of economy of movement and the oppositional pulls of one part of the body against another part; especially the archaic style of movement which shaped a Graham dancer's body and movement.

There was a quickening of creative innovation in movement; impossible unpredictable twists; you were made to *think*! It was not easy.

Louis would say,

> move the leg to the back . . . more . . . now twist the movement . . . pull the arms around . . . show the tension . . . be daring.

You worked for perfection with Louis Horst; his critical analysis was unerring and unnerving. In certain forms one movement evolved out of the previous movement—organic—but in other aspects of art—dance studies, the body became a device for strange design—distortion—to get away from what Doris Humphrey always described as the "boring quality of symmetry".

It was a completely new way for me of creating. Firstly, you composed within the structure of counts; when the movement plan and characteristics of the study were completed, *then* music and emotion were added. You were given the opportunity to collaborate with a composer and perform your dance composition to original music, then the mood or emotional quality was added. One based the creative workings of the compositions on manipulation of thematic material developing the infinite possibilities of movement.

This approach stimulated experimentation and discovery into the practise of diverse movement ideas; it abstracted the essential from the selected materials or themes, applying the essence of the meaning to the contemporary world. We were constantly reminded by Louis Horst that "there had to be a complete absorption with the materials of one's craft".

MERCE CUNNINGHAM

One had to be sure-footed when understanding and adjusting to the ideas underlying the movement of Merce Cunningham; to be aware of momentum, movement relationships, pertinent silences, co-existence of individual differences; the delineation of the human body; the de-coding of time structures and spatial group relationships; the validity of moving in time and space . . . "the body design and movement of Merce Cunningham was perfect archaic", said Louis Horst.

One always felt the zest of movement with Merce; of the body moving as if on hinges; the torso turning against the legs; the arms framing the movement or in contradiction to movement or time changes, generating movement options and possibilities.

[1] American Dance Composer, Connecticut College, New London, U.S.A.

In the design for a phrase there was freedom of creative choice within a structure; one part of the body moving slowly, another part moving fast, freely; leap, fall, quiver, stand still, sense of expectancy, speed of the steps; release of the back, planal consciousness; long parallels of measurement. There was a fresh approach to movement; one felt unencumbered; one could find a new freedom through change, or doing away with one's limitations. Merce advised me to "look into The I Ching or Book of Changes".[1]

John Cage, composer, would play the piano during a dance class—but the music was separate from the dance—it co-existed.

As John explained "each musician, actor, dancer, works on what they have to do in the piece. It depends on which move is made as to the result, so that sometimes one will get a very different set of results; if a good move is made it can be repeated, but it may never occur again; the chance element can operate unsatisfactorily so that the moves that are made do not result smoothly. Chance is very risky!"[2]

DORIS HUMPHREY

The next dance personality to further inspire me was choreographer Doris Humphrey. The following notes are from the opening session in February 1958 of her advanced classes in choreography at the Juilliard School of Music (Dance Division). The question entered my mind then, "How does one teach choreography?" ... but Doris had already begun to speak to us, sharing her experience, principles and values on dance and her perspective of choreography.

since the earliest times man has danced and composed dances handing them on from one generation to the next; there have been examples in the past of artists annotating their ideas for dances; Petipa left explicit directions to Tchaikovsky for the music of the Nutcracker Suite; Arbeau minutely described dances in Orchésographie;

perhaps because the dancer thinks with his body and the focus has been on the sheer physicality of the art, there has been too little written in the past on the theories or analyses of creating for dance;

from now on I would encourage all those who can write about dance, to do so; after the upheavals caused by the First and Second World Wars changes took place in the way man looked at the world.

The modern dancers, particularly in America, questioned the meaning of their dance—they stressed that it was a serious art form and they were pre-occupied with movement potential and its unlimited possibilities ... searching for original movement in every direction ... they craved a way that would direct their inspiration—a coherent unity for diverse ideas, visions, feelings, movements ... there was a trend among choreographers for a form—an organisation of materials.

As Walter Sorell[3] states: "Doris Humphrey and Louis Horst both stressed the

---

[1] *The I Ching or Book of Changes, Vol. 1 and 2*—The Richard Wilhelm Translation, rendered into English by Cary F. Baynes. Foreword by C. G. Jung. Routledge and Kegan Paul Ltd, London, 1960.

[2] Conversations with Merce Cunningham and John Cage—Cunningham Studio of Modern Dance, New York, 1960.

[3] Walter Sorell, Dance Critic, Author, Poet, attended these sessions watching and assimilating the process of the craft.

artistic elements of design, dynamics, rhythm and gesture choosing different ways of manifestating and organising their materials; Doris explored the elements extensively. I welcomed the opportunity to be part of her approach in creating a composition''.

We made our statement beginning with a simple walking pattern. 4/4 one bar phrases . . . extending into runs, hops or leaps in the three main directions: diagonal, side, circular; with a jump or turn; the phrases lengthened into sequences. Miss Humphrey asserted that dynamics are the life-blood of the dance; symmetry is life-less; unison to be used sparingly; design delineates the shape, the intention; opposi-tion is the strongest line one can make, suggesting force; rhythmic patterns give colour and variety over all is the form, the shaping of the phrases within the struc-ture. Far from inhibiting one's creative flow we became more resourceful; develop-ing the facility to invent; we were free to move in our own dance styles; the creative results were diverse with some astonishing combinations.

Leaning forward in her chair, her slender frame erect, pale red-gold hair crowning an expressive face, she commented in detail on every phrase of movement; encour-aging our individual creativeness[1] and with a senses of the theatrical possibilities of movement materials for the stage and performing . . . one's efforts either expanded or diminished according to one's creative potential. She would say "what are you going to dance about? It should lend itself to the movement.''

I am reminded of the words with which she reaffirmed the efforts by the dancers in these sessions "these are the ingredients or tools for use in the craft of composi-tion *but* they will not make you a choreographer; that is a gift . . . you must have the creative spark; choreographers are special people''.

I think that her words about the general position of the choreographer in the world of aesthetics is of concern to those who create. This is an excerpt from Advice to Young Choreographers by Doris Humphrey in the Juilliard Review—Spring 1956, New York.

> You should always remember that the dance is the only art without a permanent record of itself, and I say this in spite of the fact that dance notation is making headway and that a few films have been made. In comparison to the durability of paintings, musical scores, books and sculpture, dance is highly perishable. It has a moth-like existence and dies in the spot-light. This means, among other things, that dancers do not have hundreds of scores from which to learn as musicians do, but must be in a place and a position to acquire any finished com-positions from a live teacher or choreographer, from mouth to foot, so to speak. There must be thousands of young dancers with good technical equip-ment who, through various circumstances, have nothing to dance, or, worse than nothing, some trash thrown together in utter ignorance or desperation. The obvious answer to this is more choreographic information through nota-tion, which is slow, or through more study of the subject at first hand, which is faster. If you, through me, can acquire some of the knowledge and skill you need in order to compose, you will be better equipped to deal with any situation in which you must depend on yourself. Suppose you were to wake up some morning to find that Fate had deposited you in a small town, any small town, or even a medium-sized city. The chances are that there would be no one who could teach you a good dance, nor any group you could join which had a know-

---

[1] Performed in lecture demonstrations, master workshops in choreography. New School of Social Research, New York; Connecticut College, Summer School of the Dance; Repertory, Life of the Bee, for Doris Humphrey, American Dance Festival.

ledgeable director at its head. But you would not be at a loss completely because you would know something about choreography and could make dances of your own. They might not be masterpieces, but they could not be utterly without value. And one more thing I shall expect, wherever Fate may lead you; that you will spread the light of understanding among the people you meet, and do your bit to further the progress of the dance either as a teacher or a dancer or, best of all, as a choreographer.

I had invited Doris Humphrey to Australia to further enrich the dance . . . I felt that she and Gertrud Bodenwieser would have understood and valued each other for their artistic and creative minds . . . both had deep human values and had overcome personal suffering to continue their art.

Doris was hospitalised and died at the end of 1958. Gertrud Bodenwieser died in 1959.

★　　　★　　　★

The daily classes with these teachers and leaders of the modern dance, increased my standard of dance performance in technique and the range of possibilities of movement through composition; concepts about the dance form that had always inspired me had been expanded, enriched, changed. It was largely due to the influence and teachings of Doris Humphrey that I began to create and choreograph. During this *three-year period* of study and experience (1958, 59, 60) I had the compatibility of kindred spirits who understood my need to search out new discoveries. I had been assisted in every way to meet the new changes, qualities, concepts, philosophies and movement language of dance and its creative forms; continuities, environments . . . to see.

I believe that my will and imagination made the best choice.

Return to Sydney. Introduction of
New Dance Perspectives to Australia

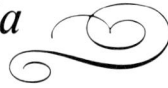

In accordance with the conditions of the Fulbright Award, I returned to Australia in 1961 at the completion of my programme of studies in the modern dance.

It was inspiring to meet with my dance colleagues[1] in the Bodenwieser Studio, Sydney again and to introduce to the dancers the influences, diverse styles, techniques of the American Modern Dance artists in such a way that it would be a living expression of dance. To provide an environment that would stimulate understanding and a positive dance response by sharing impressions, anecdotes, philosophies and as much new dance material as possible of the language of the body in movement and the theory and practice of composition.

To accomplish these new ideas and ways of moving, the dancers needed to experience and adapt to the elements and concepts of the new techniques, in terms of the suitability of their own bodies and the organisation of the movement. Central to the intentions and actions, was the immediacy and urgency of communicating to them these new idioms of expression. By an intense learning process we established a new awareness of "what dance is", by the physical certainty of the body moving and the necessity of experiencing the source of these movements, as well as communicating viewpoints and feelings about the new and different dance forms, styles, subtleties and complexities of the language of the techniques.

Through a deep preparation and consciousness of body movement the dancers proceeded to articulate the dynamic shape of the dance of Martha Graham, the emphasis and interpretations; "the daring of the fall"; the increased mobility of the spine as it allowed the movement to release and spiral across and around the back and to balance precariously in the contraction-sit; or to direct their energies across the floor in a series of walks, runs, triplets, turns and leaps.

Spatial relationships, shifting centres of balance, parallelisms created a changing network of movement connected to the dance of Merce Cunningham.

Compositional devices shaped the creativity of the group. The response to the elements and structures of the choreographic method of Doris Humphrey was demonstrated in a variety of creative expressions of movement possibilities and groupings and the discovery of their own personal creativeness. This took the form

---

[1] Margaret Chapple, Keith Bain, Eva Nadas, Helen Lisle, Debbie Thompson; joined by Peggy Watson, Lesma von Sturmer, Ruth Galene. Other dancers, students, teachers, educators.

13

of articulating through the creative practise of assignments, a range of interesting and inventive compositions based on developing dynamic, rhythmic, spatial and gestural themes and their progressions.

These dancers formed the nucleus of choreographies Day of Darkness and Éloges; deepening the interpretation of the lyrical and dramatic themes, by their own innate abilities as dancers; assimilating the adaptation of the new movement materials, the phrasing, tensions and shape in accordance with the subsequent choreography.

Other choreographies were: The Forest; Ritual for Dance, Play and Magic; L'Isle Joyeuse; all composed for Fort Street Dance Group, young dancers of outstanding ability, chosen from the programme of dance which I implemented at Fort Street Girls' High School, Sydney, in 1963–1974.

To heighten or enhance a moment in the unfolding of the subject matter, I drew on or adapted movements from the theatre dance forms that I had experienced; the juxtaposition of bodies through group forms; the expression of the back in the walk or the dynamic beat echoing through the pelvis.

These movements and many more from the creative artists known to me, were valid in so far as they evoked the spark of imagination to express a viewpoint, later to be more fully expanded in the reality of ideas through content and form.

Without the presence and support of the dancers and the existence of Ballet Australia I would not have been able to achieve my creative developments. This non-profit organisation, Ballet Australia, directed by Valrene Tweedie, was aimed at creating an outlet for the gifts and talents of young choreographers in collaboration with dancers, musicians, stage and costume designers; an integration of the arts.

Under the auspices of this new active structure, choreographers were assisted in every way financially and artistically, to create original dance works for performance in the professional environment of the theatre; from these artistic experiences some artists have continued to bring their art to maturity through choreography and creativity in dance. Ballet Australia was fundamental to the development of aspiring Australian choreographers.

CHOREOGRAPHIES

Éloges (Praises)	Elizabethan Theatre, Sydney	1962, 1964
Day of Darkness	Elizabethan Theatre	1962, 1964
Improvisations	Cell Block Theatre, Sydney	1970
L'Isle Joyeuse	Cell Block Theatre	1970
The Forest	Cell Block Theatre	1970
Ritual for Dance, Play and Magic	Orpheum Theatre, Sydney (Third Choreographic Competition)	1971

Creativity is a means of communication. Once an idea ignites the imagination, the longing or search for ... "a state of experience or existence ..."[1] is again fulfilled. We begin, develop and complete our vision and action. The flow of ideas have been expressed through dance composition. In due course there is a new discovery of insights which need re-forming, to emerge as a unity through another idea, then the cycle of creativity begins all over again.

[1] *Creativity. The Magic Synthesis*. Silvano Arieti. Basic Books Inc., Publishers, New York, 1976.

CHOREOGRAPHIES

Éloges

> And I believe that Arches, Halls of ebony and tin were lighted every evening at the dream of the volcanoes, at the hour when hands were joined before the idol in gala robes.[1]

Canzona (song) the maiden goddesses prepare for the coming of the Chosen One. She is invested with the sacred cloth of gold, symbol of glory and praise, and is carried off by the celebrants.

Sharagan (Hymn of Praise) two voyagers embark on a journey into the unknown. The Figure of Age and Destiny shapes their fate, and they are forced to part—in their aloneness they are purified.

Through an encounter with the maiden goddesses the threads of immortality are delivered unto them.

THE MAIDEN GODDESSES: Margaret Chapple, Helen Lisle, Eva Nadas, Debbie Thompson, Peggy Watson.

THE CHOSEN ONE: Ruth Galene

THE FIGURE OF AGE AND DESTINY: Lesma von Sturmer

THE VOYAGERS: Coralie Hinkley, Keith Bain.

ÉLOGES

Canzona

The light illuminated the five dancers in white; beings who for a few fleeting moments will entice us into the life of the imagination.

Like carvings on a stone relief, the figures are seated one behind the other in a diagonal line; the bodies curve forward to the floor and upward; slow ... successional flow.

Arms trailing like wings;

Lifting slowly   hymeneal

opening

through the face   moving in perfect unison

The heads crowned with gold strands; aureole.

The ground swell of movement

Space between the dancers so that the plasticity of the forms will emerge more expressively—shaping the body in an abstract way, each dancer a nucleus of organic vitality—overall a unity of serenity.

An arm contracts into the side of the torso, then fills the space with its extended curve;

[1] *Éloges* (Praises). St John Perse. Bollingen Series LV. Pantheon Books Inc., New York, 1956.

Éloges (Praises), Helen Lisle, Keith Bain, Coralie Hinkley, Lesma von Sturmer
Photograph: Denise Fletcher

The curves undulate; lightly balancing on the rhythmical texture of the ancient chants in the music.

Spiral configurations

curves and angles implicitly defined, infusing their movements with light, shifting ... to the back contraction;

The sculptural movement images crystallise; symbols of an unattainable existence, the dancers go beyond themselves into the realm of the celestial world—to realise their own creative being.

Like beaten gold their arms move sinuously, elbow, wrist, hand. The archaic spirit lies in the tensions of the final balance on the point of the elbow and the knee; oppositional pulls; the body twists, suspends ...

Submit to the daring tilt of the body curving into the spiral balance ... around the back ... contraction of the pelvis ... releasing through the back ...

Éloges, Ruth Galene
Photographs: Denise Fletcher

18

Swiftness of arrows in flight.

"The eternal spirit's eternal pastime—shaping, re-shaping."[1]

The curves of the body are mirrored in the high circles of the legs; the dancers, symbols of goddesses, move towards "The Chosen One".

In a slow and deliberate dance of veneration, four of the white-clad figures carry the gold mantle; stately walks, wide second positions, long undulations; leg extensions, lunges with the arms extending into oppositional lines; all interwoven with the folds of this ribbon of gold.

"THE CHOSEN ONE"	RUTH
pristine	
darting like a flame, poised;	the red hanging curtain floating upwards;
Turns, plies, arabesques,	
little steps, fluttering fingers	delicate tracery of the body in parabola;

She runs with the gold mantle

tirelessly across the floor.

A glittering snake, rhythmic coils fill the space;

The four dance figures or Goddesses approach "The Chosen One".

They stand with weight on one leg and the working leg lifted in retiré; the torso tilts towards the leg, the opposition hip is thrust out;

Ruth as "The Chosen One" releases from a low turn into arabesque; she kneels, contracting;

The group make the transition towards Ruth investing her with the gleaming gold of the mantle, symbol of glory, praise; she is lifted and carried off.

The lyric mood changes to one of mystical intensity;

"Beauty is truth, truth beauty—that is all
Ye know on earth, and all ye need to know".

Sharagan

See, I have given you wings on which to hover, uplifted high above earth entire and the great waste of the sea, without strain.[2]

Smooth white surface

overhung with white silken cords

[1] *The Poetic Image*. C. Day Lewis. Jonathan Cape, London, 1947.
[2] *Ode to a Grecian Urn, John Keats*. Edited by Norman Hepple, Cambridge University Press, England, 1931.

VOYAGERS   Coralie   in profile

                                     Keith   facing front

Our internal space is organic

a sense of voyaging, growing, moving, preserving the human image; our external shape, abstract, linear, archaic, two-dimensional. We expressed our dream through the symbolic use of ropes . . . a sail . . . a desire to leave our earth-bound existence and find ourselves in another sphere, perhaps spiritual.

Within this frame of white ropes the voyagers create a changing image of moving lines; intersections, edges, angles, walls, tensions; they define their shapes and space preserving close ties with each other.

We enter cave after cave of light, hollowed out forms in our transparent structure; buoyant on the moving tide;

Our hands reach for the corners of the ropes; we anchor them between our feet; the bodies bend and the third rope completes a curve in the space; ropes tilt obliquely as we travel to side.

Close the space;

Feel the weight of the frame as we press the rope downwards;

Expand the space!

Penetrate the symmetry or asymmetry of these prolongations, fragments of irregular geometrical shapes!

Change the shape and size!

From ankle to wrist we are entwined in smooth loops.

The shifts through the backward walks, shaping the body into the deep contraction, pulls the rope frame tightly; stepping back into an oppositional design we complete the tension; the white lines are outstretched through the arms into a horizontal aspect.

Our balances, fleeting, shifting as we manipulate the sails.

The couple begin their voyage, enmeshed in the rope strands; neck, ankle, wrists. Keith leads in the walks, pulling his partner behind him; in the last movements of their progress forward the body designs dissolve into the arcs of the side contraction.

We show the shape of birds.

In an unbroken cycle of movement our quest is towards the figure of Age and Destiny;

"We are swept with the wind, white sails lost".[1]

Our inner life shaken . . . we have been moving on a tranquil sea;

---

[1] *Greek Lyrics. Translation by Richard Lattimore.* University of Chicago Press, U.S.A., 1955.

Now wheeling,

Now wandering freely

I arrange the white ropes on the floor—island;

Our dance, strange

Intense, personal,

> "When the woman's body seemed like a boat lifted over the powerful exquisite wave of the man's body, perfect for a moment, and then once more the slow intense, nearer movement of the dance began."[1]

Expectations died away

Tenuous contact

We fall back into ourselves

> "I have stretched ropes from steeple to steeple; garlands from window to window; golden chains from star to star, and I dance."[2]

Music change

rhythms of ancient chants

and modern polytonality

constant interplay of rhythms

    music   dance

The three goddesses enter   DANCERS

                                                    Margaret

                                                    Eva

                                                    Peggy

their dancing bodies leaping

circular kick turns

travelling steps

"activity of the upper body   arms opening from inside to outside".

Momentum of movement increasing.

> "You moved, in the light of the streaming blue of your limbs"[3]

sense of freedom   ecstasy!

[1] *Twilight in Italy*. D. H. Lawrence. Penguin Books, England. Reprint 1981.
[2] *Illuminations, Arthur Rimbaud*. Translations by Louise Varese. New Directions Paperback. New York, 1957.
[3] *Éloges*. St John Perse. Bollingham Series LV. Pantheon Books Inc., New York, 1956. Performed on A.B.C. Television (Channel 2), 1962, directed by Bill Bain.

The three empyrean figures re-enter;
Coils of white ropes dangle from their
arms;

The goddesses float them into shapes;   The threads of immortality

                                             Figure of eight, loops, sinuous curves;

One by one the goddesses unravel the ropes, radiating out along diagonal paths;

THE FIGURE OF AGE AND DESTINY   Lesma

Slowly, she walked; a figure of renewal; carrying the golden branches, symbol of
power;

She lifts up the branches, vertical

Endless diagonals

Continuous circles

Geometrical shapes

The figure moved within the planal designs against the front of the stage.

A long drawn out resonance

   The Voyagers temporarily blinded are led to the rostrum by the figure of Age and
Destiny

Lesma bestows the white ropes on the two figures;

The Goddesses lift both ends of the ropes;

The threads span the space from low to high;

Unity is achieved

PRAISES flow between the two sources of our earthly and heavenly existence.

DANCE NOTES

Éloges was an affirmation of a cyclical form in which dancers seek tran-
scendence through celestial harmony and immortality. The movement
passages in Canzona (song) were selected from the fluid, poetic imagery of
dance language of Martha Graham.
   Through the elegant shape and synthesis of floor movement, body
design and rhythmic sequences, the quality of an essence of purity and
spontaneity of intention was retained.
   AREVAKAL (the coming of the Sun), the music is by American composer
Alan Hovhaness.
   Influenced by the musical materials and modes of expression in Amenian liturgi-
cal and dance music, he evoked the simplicity and fervour of the harmonic and
rhythmic textures of the ancient chants; strangely contrasting this idiom with
modern rhythmic and contrapuntal devices. His score for Concerto for Orchestra or

Arevakal was not composed for the dance work, Éloges; I was given special permission by Alan Hovhaness to use the composition for the choreography. I liked the expressive element of mystic ritual in the music, which is the archaic source of the dance work.

Day of Darkness

The inspiration for DAY OF DARKNESS came from the tragic play The House of Bernarda Alba by Spanish playwright Frederico Garcia Lorca.

The sun shall be turned into darkness and moon into blood[1]

Augustias—eldest betrothed to Pepe el Romano		Margaret Chapple
Magdalena: melancholy one		Eva Nadas
Martirio: the jealous one		Peggy Watson
Adela: the beautiful youngest daughter in love with Pepe		Helen Lisle
Bernarda Alba	mother	Coralie Hinkley
La Poncia	servant	Lesma von Sturmer
Pepe el Romano		Keith Bain

Tempters amd Mourners
Allan Coles, Janelle Cust, Edith Cochrane, Kleber Claux, Ruth Dunn, Marie Innes, Debbie Thompson, Michael O'Reilly.

Acolyte   Debbie Thompson or Diana Banks

DAY OF DARKNESS

Although as from a prison walled with hate, each from his own self labour to be free. The world yet holds a wonder, and how great life is lived now this comes home to me, but who, then lives it?[2]

A dramatic work depicting the sexual frustrations of women in a repressive environment.

The mother, Bernarda Alba, and her four unmarried daughters wait for the visit of Pepe el Romano, an eligible suitor. Each of the daughters longs secretly to be chosen by Pepe.

Aversion to their life in that house is expressed through conflicts and passions, consequences and the inevitability of their fate.

[1] Joel 2: 13.
[2] *Poems, The Book of Hours*. Rainer Maria Rilke. New Directions. Third Printing, U.S.A., 1944.

"Wintering in a dark without windows at the heart of the house."[1]

MOTHER

    Bernarda Alba   Coralie

DAUGHTERS

    Augustias   Margaret

    Magdalena   Eva

    Martirio   Peggy

    Adela   Helen

The four daughters

sit on white chairs with apparent calm and diligence.

                    Expressions of

                    melancholy, resentment,

                    longing, inward despair

    They stitch, embroider   bridal veil, trousseau

    weave, fold caress   laces,

Augustias; fan with blue and green flowers, tapestry.

Bernarda; austere, dominating.

A time of mourning, Bernarda Alba's husband has died.

"We'll act as if we'd sealed up doors and windows with bricks . . . Meantime, you can all start embroidering your hope-chest linens".[2]

                 They endure

"Eye, the cauldron of morning"[3]

The daughters see their desires vibrating in the bodies of the grotesque tempters.

No Piety   Like poison the movement is sensuous,

                     evil—on the breast-gold snake—motifs.

The male tempter . . .

Wide plié second, strong thigh muscles beneath red and yellow skirt; bodies bend; mouths stretch open; silent cries, fingers spread like a fan.

Bernarda Alba, proud, oppressive, austere, wearing heavy black dress.

Augustias, Magdalena, Martirio, Adela submit, yet long secretly for life;

[1] *Ariel Poems*, Sylvia Plath. Faber and Faber, London, 1968.
[2] *House of Bernarda Alba*. Frederico Garcia Lorca. New Directions Paperback. No. 52, New York, 1955.
[3] *Ariel Poem*. Sylvia Plath. Faber and Faber, London, 1968.

Day of Darkness, Peggy Watson, Margaret Chapple, Helen Lisle, Eva Nadas
Photograph: Denise Fletcher

Day of Darkness, Eva Nadas, Keith Bain
Photograph: Denise Fletcher

Day of Darkness, Margaret Chapple, Helen Lisle, Peggy Watson
Photograph: Denise Fletcher

Day of Darkness, Coralie Hinkley, Lesma von Sturmer
Photograph: Denise Fletcher

Day of Darkness, Helen Lisle, Coralie Hinkley, Margaret Chapple, Peggy Watson, Eva Nadas
Photograph: Denise Fletcher

"We stand round blankly as walls"[1]

desires must be repressed, not
"itching for a man's warmth"[2]
silence the gossip of the villagers!

Bernarda will marry her daughters to the men whom she feels are their equal

"Women in church shouldn't look at any man but the priest ... and then only
because he wears skirts"[3]

[1] *House of Bernarda Alba.* Frederico Garcia Lorca. New Directions Paperback, No. 52, New York, 1955.
[2] *Ibid.*
[3] *Ibid.*

The hand becomes a fan.

Vanity, gossip, mantilla   thorns

LA PONCIA   Bernarda's servant   LESMA

"Whole days of peeking through a crack in the shutters to spy on the neighbours and carry the tale;

and curse her!

may the pain of the piercing nail strike her in the eyes"[1]

Disrupt the existing order of provincialism.

Augustias pushes Adela closer to Poncia of the double forked tongue;

cower! Magdalena   mouths open; mime the tale of the illicit love of a

crouch! Martirio   village girl;

Seize the bridal veil!

Augustias and Martirio rend, slash, tread, fragment.

Rush to the window, Magdalena, shake your fist! Adela pushes against the door; developing her leg back, curves her body against its frame as if to escape;

Straddle the chairs   Poncia!

Reveal to us whispers and mysteries of true love;

they cross themselves

Women of the house   veil your face

Plié second   Walk   turn

wide fourth   vibrate the hand—the fan

release back

exchange confidences!

Welcome to the guest

PEPE EL ROMANO   KEITH

in the Sarabande   Spanish feeling

slow, stately dance

grave; certain religious fervour

Pepe . . . chosen by Bernarda; husband for Augustias, her eldest daughter.

but

in the duets the sisters vie with each other for the love of Pepe;

[1] *Ibid.*

Augustias, Pepe

        cold hard motion;   straight lines, uneasy partners;

Bernarda lifts the veil to reveal Augustia's face . . . Pepe turns away.

Magdalena   Eva

Magdalena, soft sensual, intrigues Pepe.

She bends deeply back   hand flirtations, the fan;
developing the leg to front

                               in the slow turns she
                               dances with yearning!
Pepe glimpses her face

   "The awful daring of a moment's surrender"

Confronting one another across stage space
Martirio, Pepe, in a bold sequence,

                               fan kicks, her skirt lifting like a disc
                               Contract pelvis; backs touch; caress.

Martirio leads him between the women.

sense of love, inevitability of relationship.

Adela, Pepe, curve in gentle arcs

Swings on his arm   Grace of the arabesque

Tenderness flows; the bodies draw near in the dance; nearer

fans, beats against the thigh.   Pink and black dresses—
                               encumbrance!

   The daughters retire for the night.
possessed!

   "Invent with your dreams, let them become the real world;
chair: symbol of immobility, frustrations;
cradle: fall slowly into its lap

You are bound to its solitude

Suspend across the rigid frame

Embrace its cold arms

Hide under the wooden legs

Heavy with the weight of your fevered stirrings

Withdraw to the floor

Side to side contract release—

the pulse of the energy pulls you into new directions''

''retreat to the white frame

Lift the solitary object carry . . . Your emptiness; Tomb!''

    The two lovers continue their interlude; following the curve of the reverse turns their movement meets;

Slowly fold by fold, his red mantle falls to the floor;

      ''My vision is ripe to each glance like a bride comes softly, the thing that was willed''.[1]

Spy!   Martirio   Betray!   Accuse!

    Impiety

    The dark betrayal of Pepe and Adela

           daughters—unleash the passions embroidered in your trousseau!— but thwarted.

Atone! Adela   ''NOW IS THE TIME OF THE ASSASSINS''[2]

Bernarda cradles Adela

    Pieta   Escape Pepe!

The lovers will never recover their human shape.

    Combat the forces of evil.

Mourners enter;

Adela will be imprisoned in the inhuman barriers of their red and black rods; She wrestles, kneels, begs,

sisters beat arms like wings

Mediaeval parallelism of the body movement.

Anguish

dark wanderings

in shame and despair the thoughts totter, reel under the yoke of their fears;

    Lifted by chief mourner the victim

Adela hangs, stretched out on rods   Crucifixion;

    Poncia covers her limbs with the red mantle,—a shroud;

---

[1] *Poems, Book of Hours.* Rainer Maria Rilke. New Directions. Third Printing, U.S.A., 1941.
[2] *Illuminations.* New Directions Paper Book. New York, 1957.

"Strange shadows stir in the darkness behind her, Her voice seems to come from a great distance"[1]

Bernarda instructs her daughters,

"Tears when you're alone! We'll drown ourselves in a sea of mourning. She, the youngest daughter of Bernarda Albia, died a virgin. Did you hear me? Silence!"[2]

They turn and walk back into the house

"To you whom to your hell my soul has followed,

My poor sisters, I give you my love and pity.

For your dark sorrows".[3]

"This is the room I could never breathe in."[4]

Dance Notes

The movement shape and design of the choreography revealed tensions and frustrations. The emotional state of controlled passion and yearning, was conveyed through the percussive beat of the pelvis in the principle of the contraction and release; tension was established by one part of the body pulling against that of another part; these fundamental elements of movement are from the art form of Martha Graham.

To intensify the characteristics of pride and arrogance, the lines of thematic movement were austere, strong, direct; a feeling of resistance in the movement; significant use of arms; one arm or both arms; no symmetry.

"If the idea and content is strong then one need not adhere rigidly to a form. One has to have a sense of physical awareness"[5] of giving power to the emotional pulse.

It was important to keep faith with Lorca's creation, his starkness and intensity; to preserve the essence of the interpretation as Spanish.

"You have to follow the blood's road . . ."

"When things reach their centres . . ."

"There is no one who can stand against this conformity with destiny. To say it with a religious word, this resignation is human and Spanish".[6]

One had to enter the situation to find out what was going on under the surface of their everyday life; to show the repressed sexual emotions of the women through their personality and behaviour—the deformities inside these characters had to be projected outwardly; they sit passively sewing or break out in explosive resentments, aggressive movements; that their pride is sinful is revealed as one penetrates the

[1] *The dramatic imagination.* Robert Edmond Jones. Theatre Art Books. 13th Reprinting, New York, 1950.
[2] *House of Bernarda Alba.* Frederico Garcia Lorca. New Directions Paperback. No. 52, New York, 1955.
[3] *Baudelaire.* The Falcon Press, London, 1946.
[4] *Ariel Poems.* Sylvia Plath. Faber and Faber, London, 1968.
[5] Louis Horst. Dance Composition Studies, New York.
[6] Notes from the prologue of the play by Francisco Garcia Lorca.

unsaid, denying the mother and daughters all sense of forgiveness and compassion . . . even grief.

The love between Adela and Pepe is rejected forever by Bernarda; she directs the women-figures to remain silent; to return into the solitary atmosphere of the house.

The expression of denial articulated strongly through the statement of the back; strident proud walks by the daughters; stepping over the threshold.

The choreography was not a literal translation of the play, but a stylised version; my own vision of life in THAT house; the pain of those who lived in it; the unbearable state of alienation; cut off from their passions.

One has to go outside the known, when creating; find movements, gestures that are unfamiliar; probe into each character; habits, personalities, secret vices, memories, dreams, ambitions, loyalties, to discover the source of one's material—to present it in new ways.

The dancers were intelligent, responsive, ready to extend themselves further into the central tragic idea; committed to working with me so that my vision became . . . real . . . not just the technical demands, but exploring, defining, perfecting, understanding each passage according to its meaning . . . their place in the affairs of the house, during that day . . . traits of personality; actions, dialogue, clashes of will and conflicts arising from their strongly individualistic roles as sisters, yet obedient and dependent daughters of Bernarda Alba.

The heavy dark-pink gowns[1] worn by the women were patterned with austere black insertions . . . the grief of their pride.

John Milfull[2] underlaid the musical score with plain song of the Gregorian chant, Spanish folk and love songs; the surging dance rhythms growing more complex towards the conclusion of events in the drama. Urgent stridency of the clarinet always heralded the entrances of the tyrannical Bernarda Alba; envy and jealousy by the sister Martirio was characterised by jazz rhythms; the male and female voices sustained the pathos of Adela's flight and the savagery of her death.

Ritual for Dance, Play and Magic

"The next work is taken from Henry Cowell's Seven Rituals in Music in the Life of Man from birth to death.[3]

The following themes evoke the ritual of dance and play, leading into the ritual of magic and the mystical imagination.''

"Ritual for Dance''.

exhilaration of the Leap . . .

"Play''

the syncopated rhythms of music and dance released the spirit of playfulness and lightness . . .

"Magic''

the movement of transformation . . . the irresistible power of the sorceress . . .

[1] Costumes designed by Margared Rieneck-Director, Genesian Theatre, Sydney.
[2] John Milfull, composer; The composition for Day of Darkness was written for voice and small orchestra.
[3] Composer U.S.A. Symphony No. 11 by Henry Cowell (Seven Rituals of Music).

Ritual for Dance, Play and Magic, Elizabeth Hunt
Photograph: Robert Walker

While giving expression to these themes, one found a renewal in the belief that dance is one of our deepest needs and expressions; that we can be transformed by it.

DANCERS: Elizabeth Hunt, Vera Bulovan, Caroline Lung, Adrienne Leal, Debbie Mitchell, Margaret Trotter, Joanna Byrnes, Barbara Wethered, Shan Heiden, Vivienne Petak (Fort Street Dance Group).

34

RITUAL FOR DANCE, PLAY AND MAGIC

Ritual for Dance

"there is always spontaneity present".[1]

Leaps, with small runs in between; Elizabeth enters first; Caroline is the last one to leap; the leaps are on the first count of the four bar phrases. The opposition arm lifts in front; stretch, bend stretch of the arm, as the body lifts extending into the leap.

"Enter from the corner across the diagonal line."[2]

Continuity in the ritual for dance—move from the two-dimensional line into a circle.

Harmony, rhythms
in the music "change"

Shape, rhythms
in the movement "change"

The next phrase is slower—longer—

The balance and the fall are slow

The precarious descent to the floor

Wide position of the legs;

Ritual for Dance, Play and Magic, Fort Street Dance Group

[1] *The Function of Dance in Human Society*. Franziska Boas. Dance Horizons, New York, 1972.
[2] The diagonal line—the strongest line in the stage space—Doris Humphrey.

Ritual for Dance, Play and Magic
Photograph: Leone Vining Brown

The shape of the body tilting forwards
or sideways.

The next movement is caught in the daring of the deep plié ... the concave shaping of the pelvis in contraction ... the immediate release into a turn, leg lifted back,

              vitality

                                          necessity

            energy

            joyousness

propulsion

The five dancers move across the space, striking through the air to complete the archaic—stance of the archer—the same arm lifted as the leg; an oppositional pull through the back and the bent arm; the torso turns towards the supporting leg.

descent to the floor

            frieze

                          remoteness of the ritual.

Each of the dancers curve in a circular pattern descending to the floor ... the spiral form of a shell—the five figures become the chorus across the front of the stage forming a backdrop for the air design of "play".

Ritual for Play

the young dancers jump,   their youth is expressed in an
hop, turn, bend.   idealistic manner.

COSTUMES: rose   buoyancy

apricot beige silk   lightness

chiffon

In the movements of the quartet there is animation.

Ritual for Magic.

The chorus, the five figures of dance, become the imaginative junction between the spirit of dance, play and magic; one by one, the chorus reach back into remembrance of love, through the concave forms of their body movement; tender lyrical expression of the music;

   premonition of the mystical imagination,

As in the spreading branches of a tree, the chorus sit in second position, face, arms lifted.

                                      Supplication

narrowing their movement the figures retreat upstage, knee walks; they approach the spirit of magic; the dance is illuminated by here charms, mysteries;

She pulls the dancers behind her . . . as fetishes . . .

DANCE NOTES

The composition was designed for ten dancers capable of meeting the technical requirements that I might ask of them; able to interpret through "imagined feeling".[1]

   To make the meaning understood through the movement—shape, purpose, gestures, "articulated through the physicality of the body";[2] using the archaic line of clarity and economy of movement.

   To move with a conviction that "the danced rite is thus a metaphysical necessity combining human circumstance and cosmic events, even though the profound seriousness of the ideal life might be masked by mimicry and play; thereby creating a spiritual connection between the Theme and the magic purpose of the dance".[3]

   I remembered a quotation by Adrian Stokes, "movement inspired by great music whether simple folk tune or symphonic theme, should have the concrete and spatial dimension of a Greek Temple". Could I move this group of ten dancers through a spatial organisation represented externally by a formalism of design? The overall device was not to be a "reconstruction of a Greek Temple" but as a principle of spatial balance for the personification of the spirit of "dance, play, and magic"— symmetrical proportions that related to the rite.

   The final compositional design was simple; a linear aspect.

   A line of five dance figures arranged symmetrically across the front of the stage (as the frieze or chorus); along the sides of the stage space, four figures of "play",

[1] Susanne K. Langer.
[2] Martha Graham.
[3] *Sacred Dance.* Maria-Gabriele Wosien. Avon Books, New York, 1984.

enter; two on one side, two on the other; three sides of the square; the focus is toward the centre of the space.

Within this frame the figure of "magic" enters, curving on the circumference of her own circle.

In the dramatic shaping the climax occurs in the first section.

"Any device is legitimate to make a dance"[1]

The groupings of "dance" and "play" have a complementary or related movement relationship.

The group "play" begins to hop in a circle, rotating their bodies towards the leg which is bent back; they change direction, and the design of the body, on the first count of the measure of four beats.

"Dance" contrasts against the rhythmic twists and hops of "play"; developing a long sustained lunge to the side, rotating the body towards the extended back leg; arms are lifted, bent, into an angular design framing the face and head.

The group "play" jump across the space thrusting one arm upward into the air as they jump—vertical air design. The chorus or frieze (the five figures of "dance") are *horizontal*—side lying.

"Play" and "dance" relate to the spatial tensions in the level and planes;—arms are lifted into an angular design above the head, palms of the hands facing outward—the group "play" stand; the figures of "dance" kneel; they relate in the flowing, curved lines and shape of the movement; the figures in the ritual for "dance" descend to the floor, one by one; the bodies costumed in long white jersey dresses, extended the curve of the turning movement—suggesting continuity;

"Play" moves up and down the stage space; light aerial movement; steps of elevation against the sustained and flowing phrases of the chorus;

A harmony of form; expression linked to the ritual.

The musical structure during "dance" and "play" was rhythmic; kinetic; accented through body movement; Movement impetus increased with the musical dynamic; it was through the pulse of the rhythmic energy that I evoked the power in "dance" . . . Transforming the texture of that dynamic into lightness for "play" . . . a fundamental trait in the human spirit, according to creative artist, MAN RAY, "It liberates life from its burdens, elevating it into the light aerial ether of the 'non-compulsory'";[2] the movement phrasing for "magic" paused, glided, touched the musical elements momentarily; the atmosphere was one of premonition, other worldliness, mystery.

The character "magic" became merely an indication of the spirit; a mercurial figure moving with strange twistings; dancing as an enchantress in her gold and silver thread costume.

We do not use the incantations nor the ritual of her trance-like state. She entices the figures of "dance" and "play" into the magic of the circle.

---

[1] Mary Anthony, dancer, choreographer, Texler Dance Studios, New York, 1959.
[2] *MAN-RAY, The Rigour of Imagination*. Arturo Schwarz. Thames and Hudson Ltd, London, 1977.

L'ISLE JOYEUSE

> It was air and playing, lovely and watery
> And fire green as grass[1]

This dance is characterized by the shifting images of impressionism.

It is a joyous idyll for four dancers to interpret the atmosphere, moods, colours and sensations through "a mingling, changing, melting of forms".[2]

Capturing the moving impressions of light and shade; the flowing, fleeting nature of experience; the darkening of the mauve tints of a half-opened water lily;

To convey in the dance images, the shimmering patterns of nature through movement that suggested impermanent forces. This visual world of reflections and impressions needed to be realised through the mercurial qualities of physical movement.

The elements of the movements were released in the form of changing, mobile shapes, evolving one out of the other; a new shift of movement; curving designs one from the other and diminishing into undefined ends; . . . of bodily rhythm registered through the rise and fall of the breath; sea-foam;

> The continuity of its form will be broken, nothing resolved, a sense of incompleteness, fragmentation.[3]

In sudden changes of direction the dancers pursued their own meandering floor designs; back and forth, to and fro; a weaving of patterns like sea-horses.

Small impulses from the centre of the body propelled the figures towards each other or away.

Arms like floating reeds gently undulated, the body rippled; the hair flowed with the movement.

The interplay of a flood of images, floating, circling, curving, spiralling, generating bright, lighthearted tension between the figures.

If the movement curve was towards one side of the body, it shifted to a new angle; from a turn the movement unfolded into the free use of arms—circling; this created moments of suspension as if poised between air and water.

A changed mood as Vera extended her body in a horizontal plane; slowly changing her shape—a crescent curve.

The feeling was heightened by a crescendo in the music—the dancers flowed into the depths of the back wave.

The movements swirled around and over the sound; bodies moving in ever-increasing circles in the space. Entwined in the lyric changing style the figures coiled inwards, then outwards spiralling to the floor into the back fall, into their reflected images . . . from under the spiral curve Elizabeth emerged; a tenuous balance.

> A lyrical piece, it seeks in soft, flowing, curved and fragmented movements, to create a poetic mood of nature . . . of sunlight on leaves . . . the transparency of water . . . a silver tree in flower.[4]

[1] *Fern Hill—Miscellany Two*. Dylan Thomas. J. M. Dent & Sons, Ltd, London, reprint 1974.
[2] *Arts and Ideas*. William Fleming. Holt, Rinehart and Winston, New York, 6th Edition, 1980.
[3] Louis Horst. Impressionism Modern Forms Studies in Dance Composition, New York.
[4] Narration by C.H. for "Choros. (I Dance)" Video, Sydney University Film, 1971.

L'Isle Joyeuse
Photograph: Robert Walker

L'Isle Joyeuse, Fort Street Dance Group
Photograph: Robert Walker

40

DANCE NOTES

The poetic imagery was visualised through movement contours, relating to the circle from the dance language of Gertrud Bodenwieser.

The elements in Debussy's piano composition L'Isle Joyeuse; dissonance, light rhythmic phrasing alternating with expressive and melodic sounds, created an atmosphere of transcience, ephemerality; the music was used sparingly as the dance hovered and dipped into the sonorities; 'as a bird skims and dives into the water'.[1]

The movement was fragmented and the flow of line interrupted to give the impression of spontaniety, 'the fleeting nature of experience'.

The Forest

"The dance figures in the forest represent MAN caught in 'unemotional motion'; finally whittled down to a skeletal shadow, lonely, rooted to the earth and eaten away by light".

"I saw in the emaciated figures of the sculptures of Giacometti, man in his anonymous state, alienated, constantly grasping for happiness.
In his frenzied search man almost makes contact with his fellow man but is prevented from doing so by a ritual killing which emphasises man's inability for communication and understanding."[2]

DANCERS: Elizabeth Hunt, Vera Bulovan, Caroline Lung, Adrienne Teal, Debbie Mitchell, Margaret Trotter, Janet Brown, Helen Fong.

THE FOREST

Absorbed, lost in their hostile world, inert figures begin to move out of their dark silhouettes; they are not passive victims—but deceptively calm—alienated from their natural selves—cut off from the experiences of human feelings.

They burn with an inner fire; their movements are hard-edged; faces expressionless; hair severely drawn back; their aggressions are hidden behind a guise of anonymity. They exist in "the absolute trance-like balance between night and day".[3]

The dancers represent the emaciated sculptural beings of Giacometti—and his conception of life—of man's inability to communicate with his fellow man.

The figures, lying on the floor, prepare to move with a silent tension.

Unyielding, these taut shapes lift and bend their limbs like levers, segmented, hollow stumps conveying to us their message of isolation, alienation, dehumanisation.

The movement statements, stretch out in time and space; slowly rising from the floor they move into their own evolvements, cold, secretive, suspicious. The focus is unswerving; a single movement of one part of the body; a definition in the intervals of silence; monotonous, rigid.

"It was a strange new forest, a place where the trees grew both up and down."[4]

[1] Doris Humphrey. Dance Composition Studies, New York.
[2] "Choros" (I Dance) video-dance film made by Sydney University, 1971.
[3] A Rose for Winter. Laurie Lee. Penguin Books, England, 1955.
[4] Of Dreams Unborn. Rae Hogan. Peduso, Sydney, 1982.

The Forest, Fort Street Dance Group
Photograph reproduced from video-dance film "Choros"

Stirred out of stillness, the back arches . . . a profile etched as if on a cameo; the arm extends in opposition to the leg; the back is raised to an upright position; an inhospitable image.

The limbs explore the space; appendages stretching away to nothingness; the measurement whether vertical or horizontal is always through parallel lines of body movement and through the shifts of the weight and is deliberate—there is no turning out.

An increased consciousness, if one arm moves, then everything else has to move; the movement line or form never resolves into harmony.

The parallel thrust of their stance is challenging as they face their desolate landscape . . . a featureless plain of dead trees . . .

They move within silence, each one regulating the rhythm and dynamics of their movement through their own inner timing.[1]

[1] The length of time taken to fulfil and perform the movement phrases depends on the dancer's own measurement of the movement—this is dictated by each individual's sense of inner timing. From dance studies with Merce Cunningham, New York.

42

The dance-movement language is geometricised, as the long linear intersecting lines of movement evolve into a juxtaposition of opposites; overlapping, contrasting, dividing, from the centre to the periphery; in a multiplicity of angles, planes and shapes.

These shifting figures partition the space and seek within their own robotised structures . . . their distance.

Their movement relationships are a manifestation of "unemotional motion; cold links to the world, inert, uncomprehending of the layers of human feeling".

I can see their inner emptiness!

Suspended in a series of balances;—where one leg is raised behind and arms circle successively reaching forward—the extended leg is parallel relating to the parallel position of the arms—the figure moves backwards into the void.

Clutching at their own emptiness they accelerate into fast runs—moving across the floor in individual diagonal directions—one arm closes in front of the body then opens—an indication to change direction; almost colliding they extend into leaps and search among the shadows.

    they gather into clusters . . . inarticulate, aliens, accuse,

        jostle.

           dislocate, emergency!

exploding with a dynamic force, limbs assail . . . the body is flung to one side . . . the torso twists . . . against . . . arms betray . . . parallel limbs . . .

erase the imprints . . .

Rapid, stilted, uneven, walking steps reflect the mechanical structures.

Then like particles of dust rising from the barren ground the group whirl away, stirred by a memory or a need, one figure remains; "the isolate".

A second figure enters the space; "the human one"; a symbol of an emotion which could awaken feelings of human warmth and tenderness; thus ridding the desolate one of a withering inner emptiness.

They move towards each other with "directness and absorption; a consciousness of movements"[1] devising lines and planes of the body that are parallel; the emotion is understated; as yet a sense of formalism in their relationship; in the carefully articulated shapes, "the isolate" and the "human one" create a tension.

Their hands stretch out to each other, constantly grasping for happiness. Light as air, suspended on the half-toe they sink with symmetrical ease into a unity of emotional expression—the forms are circular—moving—as in the growth and change of bodies; seed; shell; bud; . . . swelling.

There is counter tension between the figures in this relationship. Through deep lunges and kneeling they stretch, contract; one figure reaching forward over the second figure who bends backwards.

[1] The Archaic. Modern Dance Forms. Louis Horst. Dance Studies, New York.

The Forest
Photograph: Robert Walker

In a continuous pattern of flowing movement they reflect their hopes and desires; looking into the heart; no longer "transparent constructions".[1]

These moving forms are made of flesh; fragments of life; becoming human.

"Harsh strident sounds of music reach out like antenna"[2]

Whirling emaciated figures surge forward to the couple who have turned to each other, seeking love;
With aggressive jerky movement of arms and legs, the cluster travels around the figures; sharp hops, accented arm movements that bend up and down and sideways; feet are flexed and beat a rhythm against the gestures of the arms.
Signals!
The figures cross, pass, re-pass swinging their leg front and back (small movement) in monotonous repetition.
Struggling to edge her way upward; exploding with a roar they crush their victim.
Blurred light

The cluster moves back into its own secretive evolvements; in their comings and goings, they are never enticed by love; they prefer only themselves;

heads jerk approvingly; limbs signal; suspicions. Eyes stare inward;

[1] Alberto Giacometti referred to his figures not as a compact mass but as "Transparent Constructions". The human body has for him only the significance of being the outward symbol of an intangible subjectivity. *A Concise History of Modern Sculpture*—by Herbert Read. Thames and Hudson, U.K., 1964.
[2] Permission given by Alwin Nikolais, American modern dance choreographer and innovator; Choreosonic Music of the New Dance Theatre of Alwin Nikolais—Hanover Records, New York.

They cross, circle, pass, listening to their own silence . . . bland brutality.

"disembodied yet animate things that balanced and tottered or flailed; as if instinct impelled and ordered all their distilled chaos".[1]

they do not see her body hollowed out:

"the crown of the head to the floor"[2]

Palms of the hands and soles of the feet still showing the marks of the human image . . . broken.

"The forest must weep and bend like the shoulders of men, dead figures inside of live trees. A forest animated now with intellectual faces, intellectual contortions. Trees become man and woman. Two-faced, nostalgic for the shivering of leaves. Trees reclining, woods shining and the forest trembling with rebellion so bitter, I heard its wailing within its deep forest consciousness. Wailing the loss of its leaves and the failure of transmutation."[3]

DANCE NOTES

Frames of impersonality inhabited The Forest. The dancers in their anonymous state, measured the sterile relationships through geometric lines of the body movement, their juxtapositions and relation to the space.

My choice for the co-existence of the movement network, the possibilitiees of change and the element of chance, was based on the philosophy of Merce Cunningham.

We began with movement abstractions; the surrender of identity by the group to show the non-human structure of their lives, meant emphasising the mechanical dehumanized gestures and movements, expressing man's isolation.

The infinite possibilities of movement, both connected and disconnected, planal designs, irregular flow of movement, spatial pathways, can become an incentive for those in terms of creating; increasing thinking; awareness; and a deeper consciousness of the movement impact.

Man's search for happiness was expressed through the silence. Increased releases of energy through the back, propelled the dance figures across the space; contrasting with a moment of stillness through a parallel balance or stance; the momentum alternated with pertinent silences.

"There must be a strict adherence to the planal designs of the body and its parts;"

A division of movement; each figure working out within her own frame, a sequence of balances through the horizontal, vertical, oppositional and parallel tensions and designs of the pulls of the body; evolving the possibilities through individual sense of timing;

Be aware of the arrangement of lines and angles of the other bodies; juxtapositions and contradictions.

[1] Beth Dean, S.M.H., September 1970.
[2] The head is directed back until the crown of the head touches the floor; part of the expressive statement that the body makes in the deep back contraction—Martha Graham dance technique.
[3] *Writings*. Anais Nin. Swallow paperbacks, September edition, 1961.

Disconnect the balances stretching to infinity!

Contract the pelvis, re-shape the torso with a percussive beat; re-locate your boundaries of alienation!

Within the clusters create a sequence of small jumps and turns, flexed feet; asymmetrical. Caroline "the isolate" is the still point within this device of conspiracy.

"Do not pre-set the floor designs for the runs and changes of direction; in the running theme you could *almost* collide and lose your way."

The clustering and unexpected travelling patterns created a feeling of disquiet, a sense of impermanence.

Listening to the mechanical ticking of a mentronome I found a parallel in the pendulum swings of the legs during the walks. The choice of small repetitious movement affirmed the characteristics of monotony and regimentation that I attributed to those truncated figures who walked into The Forest.

Introduction to Stories-in-Dance Composition

THE STORIES-IN-DANCE, are expressions of ideas crystallized through the process of creating into dance compositions.

This succession of dance experiences was accomplished with tertiary students in Teacher Education[1] as part of Special Studies. Dance and composition were an elective component of this programme.

The students perceived creativity as an enriching aspect of human development; a unique value producing original, imaginative, expressive forms in art, the province of which should be available to every human being.

Each student in Special Studies, shared a need to move and create, electing to renew and extend their dance commitment by engaging in the following creative compositions. They assimilated the ideas by interacting with sensitivity, to the intense activity of the creative effort.

Previously the students had been introduced to dance and creativity in units of work, as part of the curriculum of Teacher Education in Primary, Secondary and Physical Education programmes, focusing on personal creativity, dance and the child, visualised in movement, within the medium of the modern dance.

The content related to studies in movement exploration and its possibilities; elementary modern dance techniques; creative improvisation; development of thematic material as the basis of dance composition.

Each group was different, varying in size and ability in terms of ideas, subject matter, imaginative insight, perceptions, movement language, creative approach, process and solution. Consequently the conception and organisation of ideas and materials and ways of creating changed. In these situations I discovered individuals with an abundance of talent but very little idea of what to do with it. It was a time of intense labour. One might have a rare spark of intuitive insight into the initial idea, but the subsequent development of content and form may evolve slowly and painstakingly.

We welcomed the situation to participate in the involvement of this process, to meet the challenges of finding a way to a creative solution.

In the working relationships, we established an atmosphere of freedom. Students used their improvisational skills, applying them to the elements of composition.

---

[1] Catholic Colleges of Education, Sydney, 1976–1984. Primary and Secondary Education.

Rhythm, design, dynamics and gesture were integrated throughout the individual statements and group structures.

Releasing the imagination, did not mean a "free to do as you like activity", but an approach which could create flexibility and a variety of ideas, so that we could reach our creative end.

One needed to recognise, nurture and *draw out* the feeling, quality of expression and personality, the attributes inherent in each individual and group.

The compositional material for the stories-in-dance was selected from many sources; perceptions, feelings, convictions which could be considered as a possible source of inspiration appropriate not only to me, but relevant and expressive to the groups; a potential idea for creative expression.

References to literature, imagery, environment, were drawn on as part of the subject matter, reflecting attitudes, observations, values which were relevant to the way we might feel about ourselves and society; part of a concern for the fantasy and real in ourselves. One began to develop the compositions with kinetic and imaginative participation.

Through these experiences each dance student could become aware of their individual differences; the reciprocal exchange of imagined feeling and dynamic potential of others; the balance and interchange of creative effort; the transience of the imagination; the need to draw on fresh material to keep the movement idea alive.

The changing breathing shapes and forms of "Mangrove" . . . descend from blue to green; on the rim of the space "the individuals" stood; dream-like sentinels circling the earth . . . all "felled".

The movement search in Mangrove was in discovering possibilities within the interlacing interlocking forms, and the dynamic life of the group was reflected in the rise and fall of the breath. Within the clusters, the pressure of bodyweight changed the group forms; a shape was superimposed by another shape.

From the central cluster, smaller groups splintered and dispersed to other levels, layers and designs. These newly formed units throbbed and pulsated, reverberating with a menacing mysterious quality, descriptive of; "their slow roots spread in mud and stone" or "men stand like trees asleep, a shade within a shade".[1]

The changes in Mangrove were evolutionary; one growing out of the other. From the large, loosely packed group of thirty dance students smaller groups of three, four, five, emerged; the new life, moving in succession, unison or in a free dynamic contrasting rhythm; the tube-like spiralling bodies pausing to enfold the shape of another, filling the space.

The focus in "felled" changed from "the individual" to "the crowd". Through the interplay between the groups the space expanded or was reduced as figures were isolated, enveloped by it or reclaimed. One designated the spatial area to which both groups travelled to establish contact, but failed, was subsequently avoided, as the action and meaning of the theme unfolded. The movements of "the crowd" were mechanical, herding together in square box-like designs; there was no separation, only tension.

The space blurred into a single oneness as one group exerted power and therefore prominence, against the other group, until the energy slowed to a halt . . . "felled, all felled".

[1] *The Ancestors; Walker in Darkness. The Collected Poems.* Judith Wright. Angus and Robertson, 1971. Australia.

The dramatic incidents based on the Australian narrative, "The Death of a Wombat" dictated the form of the composition. Space was needed in the floor patterns, changing rhythmic combinations and large group design (thirty dancers). The valiant but unsuccessful efforts by the dingo, kangaroo and wombat were heightened by the well-defined mass formations of the fire-chorus (a unified group), blocking all attempts by the animals to escape to freedom and safety.

Each encounter was separate, expressive of the spirit, atmosphere and events in the story.

Ideas were related to an element of human experience. In the world of The Jumblies the strange awkwardness of their games revealed flashes of human eccentricities—their movement was asymmetrical and strange design. The play of fads, tricks, excesses was suggested in the humour of their boisterous dancing steps. The kinetic capacity was extended in particular ways of moving to project these oddities.

"a crumb of bread" was concerned with social content. The figures of the hungry children travelled around as a group by the simple action of walking and the resolute tread of marching. The large group divided into smaller groups and with a partner supported those that fell down; often lifting and carrying one another. Heads bowed, bodies drooped to the floor, the design suggested futility and despair; this feeling was further evoked by the image of the frail movements of the fingers picking at "a crumb of bread".

The soothsayer or figure in white with long extensions of movement—glides, floats, circles, re-creating the fading images of our dreams. These inane shapes are only interested in amusements, entertainments, spectacles; when their piteous laughter has been assuaged, they withdraw into their world of half-formulated gestures in La Fête.

As students, their awareness was to free the spirit and find an expression of individual personality. To experience the potential of creative thinking, of expanding possibilities in movement and greater pride in creative effort. By participating in the life of the ideas and their forms of expression, they developed more understanding of the nature of creating, of the way one may perceive! They reached out for a more fulfilling life of quality against the cipher-like existence of the non-creative.

The most significant concern was to find for themselves the source of their own inspiration.

As teachers ... "To use it in the service of others"[1]

To bring their own gifts to creative teaching and with long leaps of the imagination create the time, space, thought for the child to explore, choose, discover their own movement ideas freely within themselves; co-ordinating physical abilities with imaginative endeavour, adding their ideas to others ... "when the artist is alive in any person ... he becomes an inventive, daring, self-expressive creature".[2]

> "Where do the ideas come from?
> allow them to push out through the movement
> It is the newness ... of discovery."

[1] *Creative Power. The Education of Youth in the Creative Arts.* Hughes Mearnes. Dover Publications Inc., New York, 1958. Creative Power and the Creative Process Texts for Creative Experiences in dance and the Related Arts. Dance and Lectures. New York University, 1960. Dr Gladys Andrews; Dr Chandler Montgomery.
[2] *The Art Spirit.* Robert Henri. (Philadelphia; J. B. Lippincott Co., 1923.) From *History of the Dance.* Richard Kraus. Prentice-Hall, 1969. U.S.A.

FLOSS

The glittering lights and sentimental sounds of the hurdy-gurdy flashed their messages to Floss. She could see the mechanistic wonders flying about, slashing the clear and pure space, spinning and tumbling, leaving trails of brassy screams.

In the past, with flesh creeping, the tender young girl, Floss, had visited sideshow alley eager to encounter the androgyenous forms of fantastic human shapes; half human, half imaginary.

Curious, she now intended to return and catch a glimpse of the strange silhouettes that seemed to dance behind the tent flaps.

Once aboard the rocketing monsters—devils of death—and Floss knew that they would work a special magic for her.

She would float forgetfully on the ferris wheel. The outsized laughing face of "Just for Fun"[1] typified the immense joy that Floss felt at the beginning of all adventures. It both mesmerised and beckoned her.

To filter the origins of my idea to the group, I found a few lines by one of my favourite writers, Carson McCullers—the atmosphere of the Fun Fairs always fascinated her.

> "Tell you what, Helen," said the lanky Georgia girl, "let's skip the cotton candy and hot dogs and save our dimes for the Rubber Man and all the freaks shows this year. The Pin Head, The Cigarette Man, the Lady with the Lizard Skin . . . I don't want to miss a single one."[2]

I remembered my feelings as a child—the fascination and awe that left me dazed. I marvelled at the fearlessness of people, young and old, giving themselves up voluntarily to the thrills of death-defying rides (the big dipper, switch-back railway); or the spellbinding florid antics of the strutting sideshow entertainers.

The memory stirred in my imagination a series of ideas for a new dance piece—a young girl's search for fun and excitement, among the man-manufactured environment of an amusement park. Her reactions are conveyed through dance movement; feelings of excitement, wonder, fear, exhilaration, danger, astonishment as she confronted the shrieks, freaks, rubbery shapes, raucous space monsters and ghosts of hundreds of fun-seekers. Floss ran, glided and pranced.

Nine dance students and myself began to create the design for a face; a mobile abstract shape; an assemblage of geometric movement patterns; the shape of the entrance to the fairground could have been a wheel, a clock face. The design was characterised by a divergence from the centre—radial symmetry; but the movement shapes within the contour were asymmetrical. The dance figures were placed at different heights, levels, angles, arranged like the rays of the sun.

The body and its parts were the components for an abstract design. Neither arbitrary not static; the angles changed as the movement of an arm intercrossed with the movement of a leg. The weight shifted to the head, feet, the back; legs were raised and bent at angles. Each figure was part of a puzzle—to create a composite design—a symbol of dizzy fun!

The surprising element in the framework were the lips; petal-like, the smile melted through the finger tips of the figure articulating the movement of the face with her

---

[1] The laughing face is at the entrance to the fun-fair, Luna Park, Sydney.
[2] *The Lonely Hunter (biography of Carson McCullers—American Writer)*. Peter Owen, Sydney, 1977.

hands; in a series of movements the mouth curved upwards to reveal a smile or a pout! Expressions were manipulated into flat horizontal shapes; lop-sided and asymmetrical; widening into the opening of a yawn, or a gash! The only hint of sensuality in the otherwise plain and undadorned contours of the face design was in the smooth gliding of the hands over the face.

Floss ran through the opening and was swallowed up—the angularity of the movement design, became more oblique, slanted. The symmetry of the smile changed. Let there be something in this piece that expresses a feeling for those who crave contact with the eerie glitter, who are compelled in unexpected ways to return to the strangeness of the unrealities of the wonderland.

The tensions of the lines changed as the movement expanded into curves that symbolised the merry-go-round. Floss leaped into the circular pattern. The dance figures devised abstract shapes, rhythmically moving up and down articulating the ankle, foot and knee; pliable, cushioning; arms were stretched upwards (a symbol of the poles that anchor the horses to the platform of the carousel).

Executing small steps she moved in and out and around the prancing shapes; grasping at the upstretched arms, her bodily movement changed to rhythmic swings; Floss moved with a lively spirit! . . .

It might be an abstraction for a mechanical "joy-ride", a guarantee for "thrills galore".

The "fun-fair" group were now transformed into a giant caterpillar—completely hidden beneath an irregular-shaped painted cloth, with only their heads visible through the holes in the material. As if the monsters were on wheels they rushed past Floss; she plunged under it, inserting her head into an opening in the covering—and now this shapely combination set off!—scuddering and skittering over the floor in a serpentine pattern.

When stationary they changed their levels; moved the torso back and forward and rocked from side to side; heads up and down; arms circling.

The animated monster suddenly ceased its movement, the shape deflated, the dance figures rolled out from under the cloth.

Floss dragged the deflated shape around aimlessly—a wounded starfish? But the compelling substance was already being formed that would lure her into the next adventure.

> This dark grotesque, this my familiar double
> I meet again among the lights and sawdust
> This is the changeling that weighs my shoulders,
> the sidelong china smile that masks my trouble.[1]

Floss tentatively entered the Mirror Maze; she knew the meaning of these images by their outrageous flirtatous posturings; an uneasy relationship developed between this mirthless group and herself—their aim was to provoke.

Confronting the incrongruous shapes she saw her own body designs changing to echo their distortions. In the "fat mirror" her shape became wide, clumsy, too heavy to move; the "reflection" from the "thin mirror" was elongation, narrow, spindle-like movement; her head tapered to a pin shape; the mirror group experimented with body designs for two heads, three legs, feet moving in opposite directions.

[1] *The Mirror at the Fun Fair. Collected Poems.* Judith Wright. Angus and Robertson, Sydney, 1971.

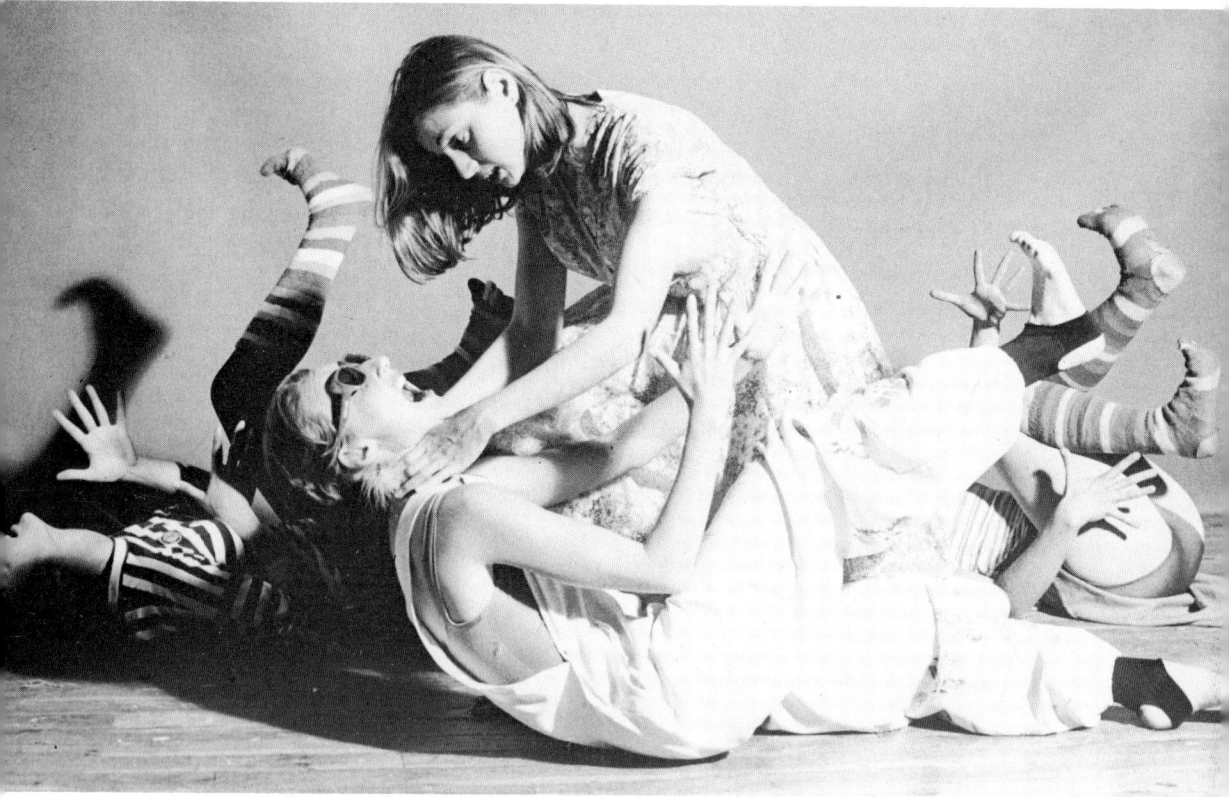

Floss
Photograph: Brian Bird

These images have disturbed meanings for Floss; here movements became weak and fickle, inconsequential flutterings, confused in her running[1] patterns she became directionless, her balances wavered; she made small, syncopated, isolated, random movement. She was no longer ingenuous—her expression of wonder had been replaced by fear and disillusionment.

The "fun-fair" group have achieved their malicious intention—they prepare to test their hypnotic power again by telling her the story of the laughing clowns.

Opening their mouths they turned their heads from side to side; she must throw a ball into each of the open mouths. She must aim accurately.

She travelled in a fast tempo to the clowns and by a flicking action of her wrist attempted to drop the imaginary ball into their mouths.

Their heads mockingly turned away—a fraction too soon—her efforts have been unsuccessful.

The laughing clowns and Floss revealed their rage towards each other—both sides engaged in a dance of frenzy—"Mirth gone Mad". All movement was centred on feet and hands—it was an abstraction of the elements of the Gigue[2]—hasty, frenzied, rhythmic manipulation of steps; tension, excitement, intensity.

[1] Based on the characteristics of the Courante and Gigue. Pre-Classic Dance Forms. Louis Horst.
[2] *Ibid.*

The clowns tumbled off to the Shooting Gallery—here they hoped to recapture their sense of hilarious fun. Their shapes were abstractions of birds, ducks, rabbits. They travelled across the space, flat and two dimensional in a percussive sequence; opposition arms moved against sharp leg movements; feet flexed; segmented movement, travelling to and fro.

But Floss was still gripped by her emotion, anger. This provided the necessary motivation for her next action; a series of devices of movement which expressed the action of shooting.

Stylising the movement of firing a gun ... the stance, direction, co-ordination, body design ... and the movement dynamic; if Floss was to be convincing in her action.

The Shooting Gallery echoes to the staccato sounds of firing. The moving targets, figures of the fun palace, and now little more than "cut-outs" created the rapid firing sounds by their percussive foot rhythms. One by one she hit her target—the dramatic focus was the head—tilting and twisting asymmetrically.

A VARIATION OF FLOSS was created through an improvisational approach with the dancers of the Creative Dance Theatre.[1]

As gifted and talented young people they had the opportunity of realising their abilities; the creative talent had not been stifled but nurtured in a liberating atmosphere of improvisation, invention and creativity.

The ages of the dancers ranged from ten to eighteen years; Rosie, one of the youngest members of the group was chosen as the innocent pathetic figure, Floss.

Each dancer had their own expressive quality. Exploring and experimenting with confidence, the spirit of enquiry allowed them to develop an individual perspective.

By thinking creatively and imaginatively we were able to develop a form for the expression of the idea; the aesthetic decisions and sensitivity of response produced, in the experience of improvisation, their own viewpoints, either independently or collectively.

Their entire language of communication was underlaid by the awareness of body movement, trusting its depth of communicative power. The concern and approach to the imaginative life of ideas and their projection into the kinetic reality of movement, were without any preconceptions, as to what the result might be. The perceptions flowed into movement images from a subjective source. Each one was able to initiate changes and to follow the movement possibilities in relation to the shape of the content. Improvisational elaboration developed instinctively into an aesthetic adventure.

The expression of speed, movement and surprise were interrelated with Floss, the characters of the fun-fair, their reactions and relationships.

The source of this improvisation needed to be realised through kinaesthetic skills, clarity, timing and the dramatic qualities of individual and group expression if the dancers were to sustain the flamboyant atmosphere of the fairground.

"Suspend all belief as you enter the glittering fantasy of the funfair."

The riderless horses pursued each other around the circle, rearing, galloping, plunging; the rise and fall of irregular movement.

---

[1] The composition FLOSS was performed for the World Conference of the Gifted and Talented 1987 with the Children's Dance Theatre of the Virginia Tanner School, Salt Lake City, Utah, U.S.A.

Floss pranced with them and was flung into the space where she danced to the music of the calliope.

An overlapping of shapes in the Mirror Maze, where each fragment of movement was passed on from one to the other in the group.

These shapes were connected by a network of asymmetrical lines juxtaposed against distorted movement images, conveying a sense of irrationality that this landscape possessed.

Losing her way, Floss moved within the strange surreal visions of the maze; small uncertain movements of the wrist, knee, shoulders, head; discordant isolated shapes and designs. The twisted contours of her hurried flight through the maze suggested nightmarish fears.

Freeing herself, she curled up under a mass of red material.

Images of space-age super heroes jumped with a rhythmic vigour towards her. As imaginary bike riders these bizarre figures discovered Floss.

She became the centre of the red monster "ride". In a frenzy of motion and explosive shouts the "larger than life" riders hurtled, swayed, swung and balanced. Floss continued to spin in the centre. The red shape spread outward . . . tentacles.

In the shooting gallery figures of cut-out animal shapes moved backwards and forwards in segmented two-dimensional rhythmic movement.

Floss then expressed her fear and horror; she aimed at the targets; one by one the abstract shapes fell to the floor; sharp changes of dynamics as the body movement twisted into irregular, angular, disconnected rhythmic shapes.

In a single movement she picked up the papier-maché mask murmuring "dead, dead, they're all dead", and covered her face.

Underneath the asymmetrical shape with the laughing mouth was written.

"Just for Fun."

MANGROVE

And now almost nothing . . . still so still.

As if rooted in the thickness of dark and shadowy mud flats, figures propped themselves against each other—a feeling of weight.

No feeling of upheaval . . . yet.

One could perceive through the imagined gleam of the Mangrove swamp, outlines of shapes barely moving, melting, "peculiar floating shapes".[1] A sense of ephemerality and expectation . . . One could perceive changes in the mounds and shape clusters; subtle changes: It was like watching the mutations of an organism or the undulations of sand dunes.

The eye followed the line of the clusters—of the folds—Concave figures scoop out the centre of movements—a sunken forest—"let you imagination weave in and out of the ghostly spaces". Music permeates the atmosphere. Long trailing, haunting sounds, flowing between the figures. Just the breathing—rising and falling—motion towards and receding; bodies lifting, and lowering.

The figures form clusters or groups in the first stages of development; they hang, overlap, bend or release the back, forward, over the figure or underneath. This moving wall lowered and raised itself, curving in a semi-circle.

[1] *A Bright Green Field*. Anne Kavan. Peter Owen Ltd, London, 1958.

54

Mangrove
Photographs: Brian Bird

A feeling of closeness permeated each group as they changed weight; "grow into the movement". No emotion, but an abstraction of the vertical extensions of the prolongations of the shape, the atmosphere of mystery and dark quality which this primeval force engendered.

The figures in the clusters developed a sense of unity of motion, anxious to achieve an aesthetic proportion and arrangement between the shapes already created and THOSE YET to come.

The difficulty lay in the subtle weight changes as the bodies moved through formulations of shape; a state of flux and reflux flowing like the life force. In our large space the groups formed the landscape of Mangrove—the seeds of a living energy; but hidden. These moving, interweaving shapes filled the space, dance figures shifted and regrouped. I moulded the shapes of the bodies, achieving a deeper curve here, a contraction or hollow there. More shape between the sculptural dance forms as if the substance was only part human . . . part nature; limbs were to become roots disappearing into the oozing mud.

The first part of the dance piece was very slow and drawn out. One breathed the music, like the long plaintive cries of the whale; far-reaching into the space, the heavens, the wilderness. The undertones of the musical composition were dark and ominous. The long, slow, heavy undulations of the forms, dissolved and reshaped capturing the sense of mystery, secrecy, danger. The feeling of a fear of the unknown.

Figures immersed themselves in the eternality of the time span. Their rhythmic ebb and flow of movement was created firstly through improvisation; intuitive, instinctual shaping and timing between the group figures. After refining and changing the pattern structures were established.

Reliance on listening intently to each other—breathing, pressure of movement—weight, inner timing, and the co-operation of the groups, led to a visually, imaginative expression of the theme.

Mangrove was an orchestration of dynamic movement changes for a large group (approximately thirty). The group forms, although linked to an overall movement design, were strangely dissimilar, depending on the number and persons in each group (five, seven, three, ten.) A dominant figure would emerge from a group, reshaping the design and movement of the cluster. The networks disappeared, fragmented, splintered, re-connected, re-shaped . . . motion unending, lifting, vanishing, enfolding—the process was slow constant and suspenseful.

The first major dramatic change in the composition was a quickening ripple of motion threading through the clusters—the teeming life that had been sheltering in the Mangrove trees was suddenly released—a "torrent of flight".[1]

They were exciting passages to compose, to find movements that visualized the images in the mind of the composer.[2] "Sounds flying; darting and squabbling of movement and voice communication; rustlings and flying from tree to tree."[3] Surging, whirling, hopping, darting, flying movements of birds after rain, swiftly flitting from branch to branch—dance figures jumped or hopped through the space; balancing on one leg so that the body could tilt in any direction, small delicate flutters of the feet and quickening of the head.

[1] *Thornbills. Collected Poems.* Judith Wright. Angus and Robertson, 1971.
[2] Peter Sculthorpe. Permission was given to me by the composer to use the music for my idea.
[3] *Ibid.*

Movements oscillated in the space—shivery grass—tensile,—glistening! I am the arc! I am the life of the tree! The arm became an arc and the wings became the canes[1] percussive movements of the arms curling upward and over, striking against the air.

The group dynamics changed—slowed down almost to a halt—the bird figures arrested their flight and in this landscape, shuffled together towards a new starting point. Decline of the old order, re-birth of the new?

Groping blindly, the clusters converged on a single figure lying on the floor; the mass take up the action again.

The pulls of the breath rhythms become slower and deeper, the entire group cluster pulsates—the shape is like a wreath or a crown; each torso contracts and releases like a river spilling over its banks; the intermittent and broken rhythms in the body movement become stronger.

Movement and energy meet at this point in the space—almost overwhelming now, the sharp points of the elbows begin to punctuate the air; bodies crouching low and arms bent, the elbows act like pistons and punch back and forth—this increased force of energy among the mass erupts. A single individual shape, newly-formed emerges, beginning with a series of gentle contractions, spiralling up into the centre of the throbbing web. This connects the relationship of the newly-emerging figure, with those in the group cluster, who surround her within their circles.

A sense of timelessness in the music allowed us freedom and space to complete new growing, changing, merging, dissolving, transmutating shape clusters. The groups diffused across the space, linked to each other in an intricate honeycomb-patterned landscape of music and movement. Bodies juxtaposed; a linkage between movements of sweeping curves and twistings, mainly at a low to medium level on the floor, so that the atmosphere of mystery is maintained.

The dancer, as the new-born "spirit of the mangrove", meanders through the interlacing of the spatial dimensions, through hollows, entanglements, elongations, never once colliding with any of the moving forms.

With circling movements of the legs, she twists, turns, curves the back around and through the openings created by the groups; a sensuous process ... emerging from the configurations with a spirit of regeneration.

As she leaves each web or cluster, bodies deflate, forms crumble; designs change in shape and size. The life force weakens. The great clusters of somnolent mangrove branches sink into the ground ... a ferment of mud and slime.

DANCE NOTES

"The birds dancing" reflected the colour and movement of the myriad sensations and shapes that sheltered, hidden among the mangroves—the excitement at the release of such energy.

I think the abrupt change to universal motion and colour alone would have dazed me; even without this sensational horde of madly dancing creatures, which were constantly rocketing up, showering trails of white water, to settle again, in fresh fountains of spray, among struggling bodies and splashing bills somewhere else.[2]

[1] Canes—Root Systems of the Mangrove—above the gound linking the earth with the trees—bringing nourishment and oxygen.
[2] "The birds dancing"—*A Bright Green Field*. Anna Kavan. Peter Owen Limited, London, 1958.

Like Leonardo da Vinci we can learn much about ourselves and our world from the natural world—he believed that "the eroded hills can become a symbol of fertility and growth—disappeared. The natural disaster of the explosion of the earthquake can become a powerful force to destroy man—nature can become a setting for our tales and fantasies in literature."

While preparing to create Mangrove I thought about the spirit of the story that I had loved in my youth—Green Mansions.[1] On as journey into the wild forest Abel had met and fallen in love with Rima, a nature spirit dwelling in the wood. He is enthralled by the young maiden and enchanted by the leafy paradise.

The author's perception of the environment is expressed with a poetic vision believing that *nature musts be vital and a continuing part of ourlives.* Abel believes that Rima will never be taken away from him: One day she disappears; in vain Abel returns again and again to the enchanted forest, but she never reveals herself to him again. Is this nature-goddess an illusion—a dream?

I reflected on programme notes by Peter Sculthorpe about his composition, MANGROVE:

> The title, then, finds many resonances in my mind; memories of a time spent among mangroves; thoughts of Sydney Nolan's rainforest paintings in which, through love, Mrs Fraser and the convict Bracefell become birds and butterflies and aboriginal graffiti; even recollections of a beach, mangrove-tree, at Ise in Japan; and thoughts of a New Guinea tribe that believes man and woman to be descended from mangroves; and so on. To me, the word itself means, in some way, "man-woman".

Some hidden power in the Mangrove gives it its air of mystery. Are we able to relate anything of ourselves to these images through this creative experience—the journey into the dark side of our soul?

Lines by Nathaniel Hawthorne revealed for me another attitude towards nature:

> Such was the sympathy of nature—that wild, heathen nature by the forest, never subjugated by human law, nor illumined by higher truth.[2]

"A CRUMB OF BREAD"[3]

They marched steadily along a narrow path in unison, side by side; this band of homeless children; a repetitive rhythm. In the late afternoon light they looked wraith-like in a few minutes they would be enveloped in softly falling rain.

Suddenly the groups stopped; in front of them was a figure, rigid and upright. They beat a rhythm with their hands, and their feet stamped harder. I understood that these gestures were meant to help revive, animate his stark, frozen body. Three or four figures gathered around to stroke his face; rub arms and legs and to unfreeze and move his body. Abruptly, the leader changed course and the bank of followers disappeared down the slopes.

There they found the lovers clinging to each other; arms and legs weaving around

[1] *Green Mansions.* W. H. Hudson. Duckworth & Co., London, 1926. A Romance of the Tropical Forest.

[2] *The Scarlet Letter.* Nathaniel Hawthorne. Penguin Books, 1970, England.

[3] *Song of the Patch and the Overcoat.* Poems by Bertolt Brecht. Chatto and Windus, London, 1972.

each other. The girl turned smoothly on her knees while the boy walked around and over her.

The one who marched at the back of the group was always out of step; one shoulder hunched and he did not walk upright, but stooped.

> who kept himself apart
> That he had been a Nazi
> was a load of guilt in his heart[1]

But he turned back and tried to squeeze between the couple, unclasping their inter-locked arms, pushing their bodies away from one another.

In their tension and fear they rejected him, and he ran back to the children's army—the lovers were too preoccupied; they moved towards each other again.

In one spontaneous movement those in the centre pushed forward and became the new leaders of the group. They set off at a faster pace in a new direction.

From my vantage point they seemed to have diminished in size—the further along the creek bed they walked the smaller they became until they were out of sight.

A small gathering had flocked to the bottom of the hill quite close to me. They huddled against and beneath the forked branches of a dead tree. One child appeared to be part of its slender dimensions.

> Who was going to aid the pregnant girl?
> Others hugged themselves to keep warm.
> I wondered if I approached whether I could help
> One child was crouching, and clutched a crust of bread
> Let no one dare take it from her!
> The circle of ragged children began to shiver
> They stared at me but showed no sign of recognition.

Struggling to their feet they drew close together and went to search for the rest of their companions.

Their steps were slow and uneven; their feet scraped against the stones and their pauses were haunting. The starving child was carried like an insect on the back of another—they were engulfed in the vaporous light.

I walked to the top of the hill and watched and waited. A cry echoed across the fields, piercing the space—then I saw the children crawling up over the cracked earth—stumbling, reeling under the slow clouds—climbing towards the summit of the hill.

The shapes of the three rich girls had come out of an old cottage to mock them. The children, as if emerging from dark holes underground, blinked, unsure of what they were seeing.

Like three precious stones the opulent ones glistened, parading like mannequins or peacocks.

They walked or strutted carefully placing their feet; leg extensions, lunges, erect body stance, proud carriage of the head; glimpses of arrogance; directed at this flock of waifs.

Contemplating the entrance of these haughty figures in the landscape, I sensed another change of mood and movement showing greed and vanity. Large sprawling

"a crumb of bread"
Photograph: Brian Bird

"a crumb of bread"
Photograph: Brian Bird

lines, deep rippling movements that surged through the body—grasping; exaggerated second positions, combined with pelvic movement and the reaching forward of the body and arms as if scooping up more goods. Small gestures of bejewelled hands to the head, face, and body as in preening; almost coquettish as they postured with the face; hips; their hands made long stroking movements over their rich silk gowns.

Facing each other and spreading wide and low in second position again they stuffed food into their own mouth, and then, leaning well forward placed more food into each other's mouth.

The children had edged their way up the hill closer to the trio; balancing like seagulls; motionless; they waited for a chance to swoop on a fragment of food.

The opportunity came when the hussies satiated with eating began to bombard this group with the remains of the food—they accelerated their quick throwing movements until there was an explosion of activity among the hungry watchers.

"a crumb of bread"
Photograph: Brian Bird

Squatting on the ground the troop of children scrambled around with extra-ordinary rapidity and agility; seizing crumbs. Solemnly the troop bent over and with thumb and forefinger meticulously poised, prepared for the ritual of picking and scavenging.

The billowing skirts whirled the three capricious ones out of sight.

A stream of light from the fading sun changed the focus—the company of children massed together in its warmth. There was not room for everyone and some were left out (pushed out).

Striking out in a new direction, these outcasts of the Crusade continued their march. Some of the children rubbed their necks, or backs for warmth and carried one another; a solemn procession in the search for freedom.

> And their sun does never shine,
> And their fields are bleak and bare,
> And their ways are fill'd with thorns;
> It is eternal winter there.[1]

Walking back along the path that evening, I stopped at an abandoned cottage; the silk taffeta gowns were hanging in tatters. Arms and legs that had moved with such

---

[1] "Holy Thursday". *Songs of Experience* by William Blake. *Poetry and prose of William Blake.* Edited by G. Keynes. The Nonesuch Library, London, 1975, p. 66.

an arrogant and swaggering style by now would be in decay; the jewelled slippers languished; they no longer danced with splendour.

The windowless spaces were empty shells
Were they a dream? Where had they all floated?

DANCE NOTES

"a crumb of bread" might have been a continuation of "The People's Walk"[1] a moving mass; hundreds and hundreds of steps walked by "humans" in a lifetime; heavy, trudging or light lilting walks; rushing rhythms of the bustling; faultering weight changes of the feeble; elegant transference of weight by the dancers; all ages of man caught in endless locomotion; to and fro and nowhere in particular.

I remember we tried out many different styles of walking in "The People's Walk"; ways of changing the weight and hence the body expression; weight on the heels with toes curled under in contact with the floor—claw-like; weight on the balls of the feet, legs stretched, a stiffening, pointing walk; weight changes through the whole foot, small quickening steps, relaxed knees (the shifting balancing action of Les Saltimbanques by Picasso).

The walk in "a crumb of bread" became an effective "dynamic", through a bold percussive step—a marching step; constant reiteration of the children's search for freedom or unsteady changes of weight expressing the state of emaciation.

Textures and rhythms of the walk would change however, depending on where the piece was performed; on a smooth floor or outside in a rough, uneven, environment.

From the beginning of this piece each of the twenty-five dance students was resolute in the acceptance of the theme of homelessness and hunger, to keep in mind the fact that this human plight has not ceased, to be aware of the unseen forces; (climate, starvation, capture).

Fine, that's the bread crumb but where is the whole loaf?[2]

"A wind tore across the body of a woman sleeping. The newspapers were beginning to scatter. The sirens of the fire engine rocketed around the block. I covered her up".[3]

"This was no breathing living shape, just an amorphous heap, but eloquent just the same; no longer concealing within the verminous folds, a human being.
   'It' shrank from passers by, who stared unforgivingly at what once might have protected.
   Crouching on the bus shelter seat this threadbare bundle of rags waited for another homeless victim."[4]

I saw the 'Crusade' as a moving narrative, a succession of incidents that defeated the efforts of the children.

"a crumb of bread" conveyed through group suffering, inferiority, oppression, deprivation and poverty; the outcast.

[1] "The People's Walk". *Creativity in Dance.* Coralie Hinkley, APCOL, Sydney, 1980.
[2] *Song of the Patch and the Overcoat.* Bertold Brecht. Chatto and Windus, London, 1972.
[3] "Observations"—Coralie Hinkley.
[4] *Ibid.*

Based on the story of The Children's Crusade by Berthold Brecht it is a moving account of the lost and wandering band of children in Europe (in Poland, in nineteen thirty-nine). Harassed by wars, blizzards and starvation, they search to find a land "where peace reigns". The theme was translated with profound force by Benjamin Britten in his composition "Children's Crusade". One felt inspired to integrate the musical experience with an individual conception for the expression through dance.

I rearranged certain incidents in the march, reconstructed experiences and events in different order. The steady rhythm of the movement theme for the poor children gained an intensity as both groups, rich and poor, met face to face; this situation evoked strong oppositional movements, suggesting conflict. Throughout "a crumb of bread" there was a feeling of sympathy for the children and their plight.

The key to the whole choreography was to give order and shape to the arrangement of the movements; to give the content a form and to select the movements that would communicate the depth of meaning.

In the approach to the idea one used imaginative thought, to unravel the images and emotions that applied to the characters in their situation. This work was not a literal translation, but rather the essence of a predicament.

My group consisted of twenty-five dance students (the Crusade had fifty-five children).

We needed to be sensitive to the feelings of the children in the Crusade—to maintain our insight into their struggles, hopes and fears.

To develop a unity with the group of mutual support and understanding of the purpose and shape of the march. To establish their identity, relationships and reactions to events that they encounter in their search.

There were variations and changes to the material when we worked on it in the hall. Some parts took on an unexpected scope and image; the three rich girls ... Greed, Pride, Vanity, used the window frames as possibilities of expression.

They slowly pulled up the blinds and caressed the window panes; then gliding a hand or back along the glass they opened the windows. With exaggerated movements the three figures aligned themselves in attitudes of grandeur and arrogance in the open windows—these spaces were their exits and entrances.

Walls were perceived as unyielding, dividing, limiting. Groups of the homeless ran, leaping up at the walls, insurmountable barriers—only to rebound and fall to the floor; or creep beside them as if on a rock ledge, cautiously. A frenzied successive leaping ensued, giving vent to the feelings of hunger and frustration.

Using the ABA structure in the composition, the theme was stated in A; the marching patterns of the homeless.

In Section B there was a contrast of material in the sequences for the figures Pride, Vanity, Greed, the style of which was based on the pre-classic form of the Pavane.

In the last Section A, there is a return to the marching steps, in different directions. In a re-statement of meaning of the theme the group scramble in a series of uncouth moves, in an effort to seize food thrown to them by the trio of rich girls.

We found a new reality by taking the piece outside into the environment; within

64

the contours and shadows of the field and hills, the group struggled to overcome the misery of their situation.

FELLED

The ash tree growing in the corner of the garden was felled. It was lopped first; I heard the sound and looking out and seeing it maimed there came at that moment a great pang and I wished to die and not see the inscapes of the world destroyed anymore[1]

"the individuals"

"Oh, I who long to grow
I look outside my self, and the tree
Inside me grows"[2]

We, "the individuals" run diagonally across the space in the succession; we continue the flow of movement in a walking rhythm in a circular direction; there is variation in the energy; fast runs, slow even walks.

The trunk in our spine . . . strong, pliable, the sap is blood in our veins. Our arms and legs radiate . . . branches. People your landscape. As you run catch the light and air, slice the space, run fast. In the silence find your own rhythms. We are part of nature . . . part of the cosmos. New life in the space, expand your natural world. Our search for who we are is heightened by finding new possibilities in the way we move. Circle the space, majestic, like conquerors. On the half toe our weight shifts forward, as vertical new growth, we move along the outer rim of the circle. We are the sentinels; long shadows; our limbs, linear extensions; resist the gravitational pull. Like the tree we link heaven and earth in our imagination; long stretched legs and bodies; heads poised on a long neck; we circle the space. Individual figures in muted colours of the forest floor, we are part of a harmonious union with the natural world; part of a circulation of creative energies. Can we use our creative imagination to release our individual spirit?

STILL, Silent, Listening;

We arrest the walks; our stance is firmly rooted in the earth; an open position of the feet; the body quivering, shaking like the movement of long grasses. The energies of movement imagination radiate through our hair, neck, fingers, arms, torso; movement flowing outward; changing, vibrant. Shake in all directions. See the transparencies of the leafy world around one, Reflect the early morning light, "shake the dead flowers from your hair!"

"the crowd"

Inside our natural environment are the harsh cities; slick people, cheap sights and sounds. They invade our life and spirit, they walk with slow deliberation into the space; the walk is ungainly, uncoordinated; with the same arm swinging forward as the foot. They are dull and myopic.

[1] "Binsey Poplars. Felled 1879", Gerard Manley Hopkins. *The Morton Anthology of English Literature*, Fourth Edition. W. W. Norton and Co., U.S.A., 1979.
[2] Rainer Maria Rilke.

We "the individuals" continue to run diagonally across the space as if the wind was blowing us; we walk on the outer rim.

Will you listen to our voice, our ideas?

We reflect the scattering of seeds on the ground; new life; winged songs; fragrances.

You perceive us with only one eye, one ear.

Will you and I cherish the inspiration of "the green man", hidden in the leaves of his or her unique and only being'.[1]

The crowd turn away.

"the photographer"

From out of the group "the photographer" leaps; the crowd bunch together clasping their hands or folding their arms, adopting flattering poses; with a click he captures a pout, a grimace, the cheeky grin or shy smile. The class photo or the family album; for "Old Time's Sake?"

"Smile on them gently. These are the family ghosts who once were persons; now they are stuck down flat."

"The photographer ceased his devilish to do. They sprang to life, resumed their ordinary face."[2]

"the game"

Released from the momentary grip of "the photographer" the mass form into lines; they stand, crouch, jump. These are the loyal fans preparing to re-live the joy, disappointment and excitement of the football game. Through mime and gesture they flash back to that glorious moment of success or defeat.

Attack, run, kick, tackle, pass, try, goal! Arms, fists, grab at the air; threaten, incite, urge, hug, flail, spur their idols on to victory.

In their own individual space they appear fragile; now crowded together, they swell to a threatening force. In this physical encounter of high-speed drama, they push, tilt precipituously and are forced backward. They scramble for the imaginary prize.

Bodies and voices expand in unison or deflate to a whisper; "Here then is our escape into Saturday heaven, our visionary flight out of humdrumn living. Adding crisis to crisis, the pulse speeds up its tempo, thudding to the climax, the deafening crescendo".[3]

Euophoria cooling, the dynamics of the group movement change; the crowd jog through the space; a sign of aggression flares.

In movements of mock play figures dodge; intercept, pass, kick, jump. Fists shake. Shout!

Trudging together in a circle, all hopes, desires, passions, are quenched as they drink; the gesture is slow; an arm raised upwards, heads tilted backward, their aim is accurate . . . they are united in the ritual.

[1] *The Tree*. John Fowles and Frank Horvat. Angus & Robertson, Australia, 1960.
[2] "Photograph Album". John Thompson. *Australian Voices*. Edited by Edward Kynaston, 1974.
[3] "Saturday afternoon Football". J. R. Rowland. *Australian Voices*, edited by Edward Kynaston. Penguin Books, 1974.

Felled
Photograph: Brian Bird

FLY!

"free spirits'

One figure leading another, leaps across the space ... they run away from the crowd; they could have been children, so spontaneous were their sounds and movements.

They play, dance and sing,

| "Whee! | swish! | glide! |
| slice! | furl! | hurl! |

splish-splash!''

The two "free spirits" run, dart like a fish or a bird.

They "dawdle, plunge, gambol, yearn, tussle, tumble, hide, glide",[1] through

---

[1] "The Onomatopoeia River". Max Dunn. *Australian Voices*, edited by Edward Kynaston. Penguin Books, 1974. Onomatopoeia—the use of words, the sounds of which are expressive of the sense! The "free spirits", Robyn and Cathy, did not speak these words—they were used as images to enrich the creativity in this section.

movements that are aerial or earth-bound ... as "the fancy takes them"; pausing momentarily in a balance.[1]

These runaways must flee, before the anger of the crowd bursts upon them. Where shall they run?
They leap, climb, clamber to new heights; far away from those with little imagination.

glide!   slide!   splash!

   wide!   tide!

"ritual of work"

The movement design for work was functional.[2] Two-dimensional, sharp, angular design; the speed and directness of the straight line.

As if on a treadmill, the mass are absorbed in the drudgery of repetitive labour. The movements are simple, easily recognisable, stylised; lifting, pulling, pushing, striking, rubbing, brushing, threading, fitting, pressing. The body and its parts, shifts, rotates, bends, up and down, in and out, side to side. The crowd punched, pulsated, oscillated. Thrusting arm and leg movements, shuffling feet, drumming heels.

Line by line the working actions expressed a necessity; a habit ... work.

Through changes of weight and levels, rhythmic movement in contrasting directions punctuated the air; faster and faster...

"Metho drinker and the white lady ..."

In her red dress she "twists like a crooked pin".[3]

Winding her body seductively around his she turns the ice in his veins to a red glow; curling her legs over his shoulder she slides down to the floor.
"His white and burning girl, his woman of fire".[4]
Their limbs tangle in all directions. The balance is disequilibrium. Toppling and tripping, their knees buckle and bend.
The derelict wraps his overcoat around his "white lady"; she crouches in its hollows; they rock back and forth; "Quench your thirst" (flotsam!).
Heaving themselves to their feet, they dance a kind of soft-shoe shuffle ... "she's my lady love, she is my love, my lady love".[5]
The "metho drinker and his white lady" stagger away from "the crowd".

"The individuals' against 'the crowd'"

Two opposing groups face each other across the space.

[1] A lyrical balance—narrow, slender. The weight on one leg, knee slightly bent; weight on the half toe; the other leg stretched forward, toe just touching floor. The body curves over the weighted leg with the arm held in front in opposition to the forward leg; the gaze is along the arm on to the back of the hand: Gertrud Bodenwieser, Modern Dance Technique.
[2] Doris Humphrey—design in composition.
[3] *Rhapsody on a Windy Night*. T. S. Eliot. Faber, London, 1966.
[4] "Metho drinker". *Collected Poems. Judith Wright, Angus and Robertson, Sydney, 1975.*
[5] Lily of Laguna. Popular tune in the 1930s.

Felled
Photographs: Brian Bird

Felled
Photographs: Brian Bird

The way of seeing was through the spirit of the individual, against the conforming, who pursue and intrude.

Run towards the crowd, try to break through the rigid formalism of their lines.

Do not pause . . . any of you . . .

Your direction is forward, diagonally in the space, bodies lifted, reach out, run lightly.

One by one run towards the person in the crowd whom you have chosen.

Continue to let your ideas and feelings flow through the movement of the running. What can you offer them? Urgency in your movement. Free them from their cold mould; the movement has a feeling of conflict, speed, opposition.

Run . . . shake the branches.

Look for "the green man" or individual hidden in the thicket of the crowd who block us.

Clenched fists, raised arms, strong oppositional movement; the mounting antagonism. Their stance is unshakeable!

Fly!

We run towards the elevated areas in the space . . . to climb . . . one by one we are carried back. Now inspection!

The crowd strut around us. Flick, sneer, spurn, twitch, prod, pluck at the hair, hem of a dress.

We feel their menacing hands on our shoulders, pushing us down, downward; we stretch our bodies upward; lift our faces; mute appeal.

Lifting our arms above our head we are stripped of our muted colours, our existence; the crowd rend and slash at us and the air.

Pitiable! We droop towards the floor, our strong and supple spine bends further downward.

Close by are the sounds of the tree-chopper, frantic at his work; amputating.

Our bodies are heaved up, supported and carried on the backs of the oppressors, who stumble, shuffle, tug, wrench, pull in staccato mechanical gestures, in an effort to free themselves.

We have forged the yoke, bonding the creator-destroyer in each of us.

My aspens dear, whose airy cages quelled,
Quelled or quenched in leaves the leaping sun,
All felled, felled, are all felled:[1]

DANCE NOTES

The group of twenty-eight dance students were divided into smaller groups: "the crowd" (seventeen dancers), "the individuals" (seven), "metho drinker and white lady" (two), "the photographer" (one), "free-spirits" (two). Because of the large number of persons, we extended the spatial areas and therefore the possibilities.

We divided the space into these areas: stage, mini-stage (two large rostrii joined together), floor space. All areas were in use as the thematic material unfolded, developing simultaneously or successively. The levels increased focus, direction, dimension; extending the range of movement in the content . . . the physical reality.

[1] "Binsey Poplars. Felled 1879: Gerard Manly Hopkins". *The Norton Anthology of English Literature*: Fourth edition. W. W. Norton and Company, U.S.A., 1979.

The cast worked on ways to ascend and descend the levels, to make the transitions clear and simple.

Contrasts in the emotional range were increased or lowered according to arrangement of characters and sequences of movement as they progressed along the different planes.

The circle seemed the best choice in spatial design for the individuals. It allowed us to be free persons, part of a small group with a continuity of purpose and a feeling within the circular design. Our focus was towards the centre.

"The crowd" moved within their own areas in the space—a compact group, changing the formation to lines (four or five lines, a square). In "the football game" the clusters travelled sideways or forwards or backwards; changing to quarter and half turns. The patterns were planned, integrating focus, level and direction. The movements were repetitious; pushes, pulls or rotations; the dynamic movements in "the game" were vigorous, sharp and fast; jumping and travelling expressively.

The diagonal, the strongest line in the space seemed a powerful link between the two opposing forces—"the individuals" and "the crowd". The former took their positions upstage in a corner, giving a feeling of mobility, heroism, yet vulnerable; 'the crowd were placed downstage diagonally opposite (near an exit corner). The groups moved into other ares in the space but this was their fundamental floor pattern for position, direction and interaction during the composition.

The running sequences between the opposing groups took place along this diagonal line, corner to corner, using the entire floor space; the fragmented running motif by "the individuals" was continued by moving onto the platforms and the stage. Their attempts to escape were unsuccessful, being pulled back by "the crowd".

When the "free spirits" were dancing their theme, the individual groups moved in a circular direction (anti-clockwise), walking freely, pausing, shaking. "The crowd", positioned off-centre, downstage, mimed the gesture of drinking.

The duet of the "derelict metho drinker" was designed for the centre—the focus is directed towards them. "The individual" groups receded into their corner of the space. The movement narrowed as they shielded each other. "The crowd" are frozen in an oppositional movement, the gesture of work.

At the end of their dance sequence they moved towards the rostrum, attempting to find their freedom—it is impossible for them to reach the stage and thus a more elevated pure existence; they stay on the rostrum, moving down towards the front near the audience; they are people with all the imperfections—they cannot reach the remoteness of the ethereal—the unreal.

In the final conflict of "Felled" the groups were joined together, couples linked inescapably, barely moving in the floor space. The "metho drinker" and his partner are at the end of the rostrum hesitantly performing their soft-shoe routine.

On the stage the "free spirits" glide, slide, run, dawdle, in their fantasy of freedom.

LA FÊTE

"WHY ANYBODY CAN HAVE COMMON SENSE PRO-
VIDED THAT THEY HAVE NO IMAGINATION. BUT I
HAVE IMAGINATION FOR I NEVER THINK OF THINGS
AS THEY REALLY ARE. I ALWAYS THINK OF THEM AS
BEING QUITE DIFFERENT."[1]

They stood close together on the platform poised like exotic fruits or plants.
Unblinking these human sculptures balanced, suspended in movement. Frozen in a
whimsical gesture; a hand holding a painted silk fan or lace glove; fingers adjusting
a rosette on a hat; looking through a crystal goblet; the character with the dog's
head crouched, hunched over weeping; another admired her pigeon's blood ruby
ring.

They had a strangely disembodied appearance.

Suddenly a mysterious "figure in white" leapt into the space. He skimmed along,
partly running and gliding; turning; twisting sideways, or down, touching the floor.
In motion the planes of his body were horizontal; he seemed to lie in the air, then he
continued with spinning turns.

He floated on; the long extensions of his limbs enveloped in the white trailing
folds of his coat—like sails or flags.

Stopping before the rostrum he greeted his faithful troupe, bowing low and deeply.
It was their "protector"—the puppeteer; they were to be brought to life! He had
bewitched this band of strolling players, who now followed him everywhere, enter-
taining the nobles, villagers and children; they looked forward to performing at
masquerades, fêtes, secret festivities and royal pageants, dancing, acting, miming;
he could lead these bizarre characters into any escapade.

Endowed with mystical powers he enjoyed animating and manipulating their
expressions and movements. Stretching up he touched each player lightly and one by
one they were released from their artificial pose and gesture, moving slowly off the
platforms to the floor space.

Today, the puppeteer had a special surprise: instead of conducting a rehearsal
with his troupe, they were going to be the guests at an entertainment—a spectacle.
The soothsayer would not reveal to them the identity of the special performer or his
act; it would be a surprise! but first he must prepare for the fête.

The troupe wished that this strange visitor would appear; droll stories always
made them laugh.

As strolling players, they presented their boisterous songs and dances, mimed the
exaggerated stories of the braggart, or in the role of a deceitful servant distorted
their gestures with sullen antics, to amuse a fine or grande dame; sometimes their
roguish ways were ridiculed. Now it was befitting that they should move with a new
elegance; it was their fête day or birthday and they deserved a special reward. They
were going to dance in the old castle as courtiers—no longer acrobats or trouba-
dours; they could visualise in their imagination the exquisite gilded decorations and
ornamentations of ivory and lapis lazuli.

With leg extensions, they walked forward, forming two parallel lines, eight on

[1] "The Remarkable Rocket". *Fairy Tales*, by Oscar Wilde. The Bodley Head, London, 1960.

each side. Arms were extended to the side in the longest possible line, curving at the wrist. By emulating the grand movements of the aristocracy, they could triumph over their former image. Parading up and down in the promenade, they linked movements and steps, alternating partners. This formal sequence had the style of the more gentle, modest and charming of the dances of the French Court.

Their feet engaged in pointed movement, sharp, concise, delicately and clearly articulated, each leg extended turned out with toe pointed and touching the floor in one of three positions; front, side, back.

The measures were performed facing each other, back to back, and circling.

Smoothly the couples executed glides, bending steps; rising on their toes; flexing the foot at the ankle and the hand at the wrist; light, quick brushes of the foot; small, flicking hand movements and extensions of the leg; pausing at the end of a measure in a flourish. No angular movement; no haste, as they processed in and out of the symmetrical designs of the interlude.

With the re-entry of their leader there was an abrupt change in movement and focus. The ensuing mood and action was in complete contrast to everything that had gone before. He ran up and down, between the lines waving his long white sleeves.

Where the troupe had previously portrayed images of aristocratic bearing and refinement, they now reeled about falling into lop-sided positions, their heads, arms and legs slanted asymmetrically; comical excitement. The troupe fell to the floor on their back, head lifted, feet flexed, watching him; their expression of anticipation changed to a strange fascination.

Stumbling behind the puppeteer was a new character, a dwarf!

This was the surprise that they had been promised.

Animated, they leapt to their feet and like revellers in a masquerade surged forward into the space, following the Pierrot-like figure and his new entertainer.

The characters sped by, winding and unwinding in a single line, leaping, hopping, stamping, criss-crossing their feet in a dance of "follow the leader".

Swathed in tinsel, satin and velvet costumes they flowed like a magic-lantern show, ending in a circle; Carnival of Harlequins.

It was time for the entertainment to begin.

The dwarf limped into the centre; in his black and brown flimsy suit and pale face he looked vulnerable.

But this ugly creature loved to entertain and to make people laugh; so he capered and spun to regain his spirits. The audience of players rocked with laughter.

Increasing his antics, he blew himself up to the size of a toad or diminished to that of an ant; he would jump about on one leg, then run on his knees, or pucker his face into a hideous grin.

The dwarf's absurdities continued at a feverish rate with tricky steps and stunts.

In search of more excitement the audience ran toward the mannikin and heaved him up into the air three times. The puppeteer was now ready to introduce to his players the second part of the surprise event . . . the mirror.

It was like a wedding procession. The "mirror figure" was covered by a silver net cloth—glistening. It streamed out behind him and was carried by the troupe.

Gyrating with glee and tumbling about, the mannikin led the procession. Some-

La Fête
Photographs: Brian Bird

La Fête
Photograph: Brian Bird

times he felt wild or lonely, but today he was happy; he had been promised a reward by the figure in white who had been so kind to him!

The cast promenaded around the room executing motifs from their court dance; hand movements, brushes, glides, pivots; they exaggerated the style of these steps; satirical. They were restless and had an irresistible urge for entertainment of a more sinnister kind. Slowly, as if in a trance, the figure in white pulled off the silver cloth, uncovering the fatal image.

Spellbound the players watched the dwarf approach cautiously, noiselessly.

The head rolled to one side . . . too big! a monstrous hand reached out as if to touch the dwarf. The feet, misshapen, moved clumsily; "it" could never dance or do tricks and stunts. LAME.

Quivering and shaking, the "Shape" came towards him. The dwarf jumped backwards, but the shape followed. This time the dwarf contorted his body into one of his most difficult stunts, as if to outwit and frighten this creature away. Who is this monster?

Shock, disbelief, increasing disappointment, sadness and realisation enveloped him . . . the reflection was his own.

Stopping crookedly and limping, he crawled and threw himself upon the floor, shook his fists in the air, wrung his hands. His movements were imbalanced.

Like a shadow the reflection followed him.

The audience clapped and roared with mirth. Mocking and ridiculing they imitated every gesture. Distorting their movements they indicated their revulsion.

They themselves were petty caricatures and suffered from deformities, hidden deep within themselves.

The dwarf and his mirror image faced each other; they leapt and whirled around in confusion; the crooked heads twisted sideways; arms and legs rejected each other with opposing thrusts; elbows and knees were bent sharply as if to break.

Struggling against each other these captives were imprisoned within their own distortions.

Tensions, strengths, oppositions, aggressions, conflicts; hopelessly entangled in the dreaded encounter.

Flapping his sleeves the soothsayer ran to the two adversaries, twisting the silver cloth he carried it to his players.

They lifted the cloth above their heads and stretching their arms plucked at it with their fingers; lowering it to the floor, stepped lightly across it . . . a symbol of folly . . . they covered the lifeless forms.

The soothsayer drew his cast of players after him. Stopping before the rostrum, he bowed low and deeply, rearranging the characters like "plants, or exotic fruits".

They stood suspended in their own gesture or movement; holding a lace glove, touching a rosette; stroking the dog's head'.

"They were a strangely disembodied troupe—"

Dance Notes

This dance composition, La Fête is based on the character of the dwarf in The Birth-day of the Infanta by Oscar Wilde.[1]

It is, I believe, one of the most poignant of his beautiful Fairy Tales. I concerned myself with the figure of the dwarf and his reactions and actions when he realises that the malformed monster in the mirror is a reflection of himself (expressed by a second figure); I found another kind of inspiration in Le Grand Meaulnes by Alain-Fournier,[2] basing the character of the white-faced puppeteer on his elusive Pierrot-like figure of fate; weaving the incidents into one idea for dance, choosing style and movement relevant to the new subject matter; a melancholy atmosphere contrasting with capricious happenings.

Each costume by Eileen Cramer[3] for La Fête, captured the image of fantasy, expressed in the movement and style.

The face of the puppeteer was painted with white make up. It glowed with a deathly pallor; over his black suit he wore a voluminous white coat with flimsy sleeves and for a collar, a white ruff.

One needed to find a way to begin; intermeshing movement, transitions and com-binations with the interaction of solo and group characters. To give meaning to the sections within the theme, increasing the depth of emotion through the inconguity of relationships.

[1] Fairy Tales. Oscar Wilde. The Bodley Head, London, 1960.
[2] Le Grand Meaulnes. Alain-Fournier, Penguin Modern Classics, London, 1966.
[3] Eileen Cramer (Kramer), Sydney, New York. Formerly a member of the Bodenwieser Dance Company, Costume Designer for dance dramas, solo and group works—by Gertrud Bodenwieser, Bodenwieseer Dance Company, Sydney.

I was becoming involved again in the act of composing, creating, making-up; at times a mystery; a flash of intuition, an illumination; a break-through (call it what you will); a totally absorbing process.

When one is in possession of this creative ability it can lead you and your dancers ... performers, teachers, students, into enlivening communication; drawing on one's experience and responding sensitively to that which is required.

The group of twenty dance students who elected to take part in these compositional procedures, were willing to give their individual attention to learning more about the dance skills involved; the manipulation of the movement, progressions and insight into his or her potential to fulfil the creative effort required.

I could visualise the images with the cast and we sketched them out roughly in movement.

If not, these spontaneous glimpsed concepts may disappear.

One needs to bring them into reality, into the awareness of the cast through the movement choices; mime; gesture and the dimension of the emotions.

A statement in movement was needed at the beginning of the subject matter to depict the atmosphere and the characters.

I grouped the cast side by side on the rostrum. Through gesture or posture we were able to translate the strange airs of the characters, their affectations and insincerities into movement. Heads inclined; one shoulder raised; knee turned inwards; a coquettish gesture indicated by the hands; the lines of asymmetry dividing the harmony of the body.

We shaped the images of these fantastic and imaginary beings, to convey the bizarre element.

By utilising his height and long flexible arms and legs, the solo character gave the appearance of skimming through the space; the fluency of running and gliding, bending the body at all angles. The balances veered off the body centre. The levels of turns fluctuated as he travelled through the space.

Using his wide sleeves, the dance student swirled his arms continuously, like flags.

The body movement designs turn inward, twisted; light, jaunty, perky hops and steps; small distortions of movements of the head, feet and legs; the lines are unequal, out of balance.

the style is strange; designed to comply with dance material that expresses contrariness, doubt, grotesqueries, incredulity.

The movement we needed to use in the character of the dwarf and his reflection or duality was asymmetry and strange design, suggesting physical distortion and emotional maladjustment.

This distortion is paralleled by the second figure reflected in the mirror image. Each one is the echo and reflection of the other; the intention is one of malevolence.

The climax is affirmed at the moment when the mirror image discloses to the dwarf his real shape.

The movement is the struggle between the two adversaries, (dwarves) and is based on Primitivism and Introspection[1]—two components of the language of dance composition.

This is portrayed by the tensions of the physical forces throughout the body, pulling one against the other.

[1] Louis Horst.

The Dragoness, by Christina Cordero (etching and aquatint)

The movement is taut, it does not open out. The inner turmoil of the two figures cannot be overcome and their strength of resistance gives way to the parallels of weakness and defeat.

The mirror becomes a symbol for the cast; they would like to find their own identity and so free themselves from their unworldly pantomimic characters.

Searching for a new awareness they lift the diaphanous cloth and gaze upwards; lowering it, they focus downwards.

The puppeteer has lost contact with his schemes, and retreats stealthily in long, low, loping walks. The significance of the mirror has waned—he drops it on the life-less forms.

For me, the posit of the creative effort was in the assertion that the quality of compassion had been expressed in the composition.

The fairy tale is a captivating source for transformation into dance; it reveals enchantment in the subject matter; beauty and ugliness. Good and bad exist side by side; we discover our imaginative powers; we can draw on the image of fantasy and symbolism, poetic qualities which enrich us and deepen consciousness.

Through the fairy tale we are in touch with heroes, nature, animals, reacting in our human imagination with terror, awe and amusement to the expression of their sounds, images, shapes and movement.

Our personal development, particularly that of the child can be explained and reassured; these are all part of the messages—the merits of the fairy tale.[1]

> each fairy tale is a magic mirror which reflects some aspect of our inner world, and of the steps required by our evolution from immaturity to maturity. For those who immerse themselves in what the fairy tale has to communicate, it becomes a deep, quiet pool which at first seems to reflect only our own image; but behind it we soon discover the inner turmoils of our soul—its depth, and ways to gain peace within ourselves and with the world, which is the reward of our struggles.[2]

COME OUT OR SHAPED LIKE AN EGG

> "The house had the shape of an egg, and it was carpeted with cotton and windowless"[3]

The source of my idea for the theme on birth:

> "the egg; calm, protective, liquid, plastic, a promise, new life, non-edible".[4]

This is an indication of how I set the idea in motion for a group of twenty-five students who felt ready to become part of this creative experience with me.

"We are going to prepare ourselves for the release of the imagination"; to experience the sensation of "letting go"; of freeing the mind; of bringing up from our interior world impressions and ideas, which may seem unrelated to you, but through the freeing process of your inner self you may find a new order, "new meaning".

find a space on the floor;
close your eyes;

[1] *The Uses of Enchantment; The Meaning and Importance of Fairy Tales.* Bruno Bettelheim. Penguin Books, 1976.
[2] *Ibid.*
[3] *Poetic writing of Anais Nin.* Swallow Press, Inc., Chicago, 1962.
[4] *Ibid.*

space, silence,
no resistance, no distractions
    no tensions
listen with your whole being.

go outside the known self;
    away from the stereotype,
discover the other side of you;
    find the sources of your breath—
    create your own rhythmic pattern of breathing
eliminate slick and superficial solutions from your thinking;

Our creative selves need using, developing, expanding; sensitising for awareness, intuitive insight, discovery; nurturing our imaginative expression, perception and communication.

Release the images, associations; conjure up your dreams, fantasies, perspectives in a new and magical way.

"Trust logic and intuition equally; the intuitive process is richer; it contains more information."[1]

Dream Imagery   Dreamer and Questioner

Work with a partner with whom you are able to communicate your verbal imagery.

Lying on the floor, relax; close your eyes; describe your sensations, impressions, images as they stream forth.

the partner or questioner asks the dreamer.

Who are you?

Where are you?

Do away with your preconceptions.

The dreamer is free to image-out what he or she is experiencing in terms of place, event, time, situation, circumstance.

If the dreamer is questioned in a sensitive way, it can heighten and prolong the stream of imagining—ask simple, direct questions, related to the theme and extend the flow of content.

The dreamer can pause, rest, continue the flow, or break through to another dream sequence.

If the authenticity of the verbal imagery is doubted the questioner must stop the dreamer—there cannot be any faking of allusions or images.[2]

She restored to the empty landscape all the mythological figures of her dreams, thinking of Rousseau's words in answer to the question: "Why did you paint a couch in the middle of the jungle?", and he said:

[1] Phillip M. Powell.
[2] Peter Barclay, Theatre Director, Sydney, 1985.

"Because one has a right to paint one's dreams."[1]

So you, also, have the right to dance your dreams; let us see the images in your movements!

COME OUT

"from your own embryonic shape

yield to your changing shape; you are sheltered by the external contour of the oval or sphere; decrease your movement, shrinking in size; weightlessness".

The only sound will be the friction of the body murmurings, shifting and changing weight; movements shape on the floor; sighs like wind in the pines.

A blind amoeba-like groping

meander your way through the space

breath will give the rise and fall of the body movement

unfurl, uncurl, brush the body over the surface of the floor

inscape; imperceptible change

your bodies resemble creatures living in shells

when you are ready, glide, touch, coincide with the movement of another

continue to move at a low level, restrict your movement or show that you are in unrestricted open space

connect with two, three or more figures in a new embryonic form—translate your movement shapes spontaneously; move an arm, leg, head; be conscious of your focus as you fuse, join, parts of your body into a sheath-like structure; arms entwines, shoulders and feet touching, create new surface tensions as you stretch in new directions or through different qualities of movement'.

silhouettes; liquidescent; the space filters through the shapes.

The mass inter-connection of movement changes, and each couple now unite in movements and slowly standing up shuffle and sway to the nostalgic tunes of Tea-Dance music.

A new character, the waiter, enters. Changing the mood, he skips and glides among the couples, carrying a large pink, paper egg.[2] He tosses and twirls it and pirouettes out of sight . . . he is flippant but . . . deceptive?

The dancing couples see the frivolous object "shaped like an egg", fulfilling all their dreams and desires.

They believe that the egg will open. All colours, sensations, secret longings, exotic odours, perfumes, will cascade over them like blossoms or pearls.

Happy to be deluded they sink to the floor.

The focus on energy is centred in this middle section of the work.

[1] *Collages*. Anais Nin. The Swallow Press Inc., Chicago, 1964.
[2] This symbol was an automatic choice. Its non-productive powers are symbolised by its lack of substance, that is, pink paper; a bauble, a decoration, plaything, not connected to life.

Come Out or Shaped Like an Egg
Photographs: Brian Bird

A dynamic sequence of movement—the contraction and release follows; the dominant expression, the confinement of smooth, rhythmic movement within the protective oval body shapes, is disrupted. At first a series of small impulses begin through the breath; lying on the back, changing to the sides of the body; the shape is concave.

The percussive pulsations increase in momentum, culminating in an unexpected release—handstand—the egg bursts! But the shock of being catapulted out of the warm sheltered environment, produces a turbulent state whereby the group fling themselves in all directions, almost colliding . . . only to collapse!

The waiter enters, carrying a tray of plastic masks. He is also a mask maker. He loves to attend celebrations and hire his creations to those who do not wish to "see" themselves, or each other, as they really are. It is said "that the mask, given time, comes to be the face itself".[1]

Three duets follow; six of the dancers are given a more flattering and individual mask. Working imaginatively their duets develop through an evolutionary process (one movement growing out of another). Lifts, gestures, and movements, signify harmony, acceptance, compatibility, in their new relationships. With symmetry in their body designs, the movements in the partnerships express solace.

The images are shattered by the entrance of the waiter, skipping and gliding around the couples, still whirling and twirling the paper egg.

With a malicious gesture he removes the masks from the couple's faces, thus destroying their illusions.

As he walks away, he polishes the egg and strokes his masks.

We are left wondering whether the couples will accept or reject their new realities, without the deceptive image of the second face.

They see each other and themselves for the first time.

Dance Notes

"Come Out" relates to the theme on birth. The group of sixteen dancers participated in the first part in smooth merging movements forming concave shapes. In the next section the whole of the body movement absorbed the rhythmic momentum of birth.

From the moment the figures as egg shells explode into life, a new and different meaning emerged. In the second part the egg becomes a symbol of frivolity, artifice.

The couples seek love but are destined to live behind the deep shadow of their mask.

While the first obscure idea for "Come Out" was germinating, impressions, sensations, memories floated and tossed about in my mind. The imaginary material was projected from the sub-conscious into improvisational experiences, indicating a possible creative path.

Perhaps this excerpt from the paper "Becoming More Creative" will convince you that *your* potential in thinking creatively and using the imagination is readily accessible if you know how to enter into this experience. Dr Philip Powell says:

[1] *Memoirs of Hadrian.* Marguerite Yourcenar. Penguin Books, England, 1959.

The first area of thinking is in the conscious mind, but the second level, the Pre-conscious mind is more difficult to understand. This area is just beyond awareness; it is not fully developed in everyone as many people are not in control of this type of thinking; it is available and accessible to creative profile.

My notion of the Pre-conscious is different from others. I think of it in the person as a revolving door between the conscious mind and the Pre-conscious. This revolving door is used during the process of creating something new; as a device, mechanism or a tool to re-code problems which the conscious mind is unable to solve into another form.

The Pre-conscious mind is able to incubate the problem, which can be deep, intuitive, making no sense; provided you are aware of this and allow it freedom to begin to re-code that problem and put it in another form.

The freedom to reach this level of thinking comes from your meditation.[1]

Carl C. Jung explains that "In addition to memories from a long distant past, completely new thoughts and creative ideas can present themselves from the unconscious—thoughts and ideas that have never been conscious before".[2]

For many years writers, artists, educators, philosophers have been searching for a definition of the meaning, purpose and function of this elusive process; imagination and the delicate balance played by the intellect and intuition, mind and instinct in this experience. On imagination, philosopher, teacher, Mary Warnock says:

The creative imagination, then is the faculty of seeing, and expressing again, the absolute ideas which are perceived as the pattern, design or essence of things. Imagination is the power of seeing things as they are, namely as symbolic, and of creating new symbols (and to a less extent new images) to express the ultimate nature of the world. And this creative imagination operates both at the conscious and the unconscious level.[3]

Imagination then opens the door to creativity; it needs a liberating, freeing atmosphere to allow the stream of consciousness to image further, achieving a oneness with the variety of ideas. "The fundamental and undeniable fact about the imagination is that its purpose, is to intensify the life in man";[4] so that we might experience a moment of revelation, as the human spirit strives to be expressed.

Dreams are a rich source of material for dance creating. They range from joyful and happy experiences to sad, frightening, surreal, often turning into nightmares.

I would suggest that dream material should be collected and recorded; you can ask the children in their class to talk about their dreams; to annotate them as short stories, poems, or paint them. Like Arthur Tress in The Dream Collector, one can find parallels in the environment in the real world.

This idea would be more suitable for older children at a certain level of dance proficiency, creative and personal development and understanding.

In certain dreams of children pain is the subject; birth can be projected as the

[1] Professor Dr Phillip M. Powell, Sixth World Conference of the Gifted and Talented, Hamburg 1985. "Becoming more creative" from his paper—Models of Creativity—Assoc. Prof. of Educational Psychology, University of Texas, Austin, U.S.A.

[2] Man and his Symbols. Carl G. Jung. Aldus Books, London, 1964.

[3] Imagination. Mary Warnock. Faber and Faber, London, 1976.

[4] The Strength to Dream. Colin Wilson. Abacus edition by Sphere Books Ltd, London, 1976.

universal shock of expulsion into the world; the egg shells are shattered with a child's face appearing in the part of the cracked sphere—[1]

"My birthday present . . . in it I found the trauma of my own birth."[2] If dream images and dream memories are your source for a dance study make sure it has movement and expressive potential. You might want your group to improvise a single dream image, or a succession of unrelated images.

You (the creative teacher) need the imaginings, sensitivity, and perception to transmit and cultivate the child's origin of ideas; once more to set the creative process in motion leading your children "back into their dream world through dance".

The music for Come Out or Shaped Like an Egg is by Steve Reich; from new sounds in Electronic Music. "I had to, like, open the bruise up and let some of the bruise blood come out to show them." A dramatic composition describing a beating by a boy in Harlem 28th precinct. This composition with the resonance, reverberation, repetition and powerful imagery was not irreconcilable with the ominous and catastrophic upheaval in my statement on "Come Out". It contrasts with the tuneful melodies of the Tea-dance section in which the character of the waiter makes his appearance.

THE DEATH OF A WOMBAT

"I saw that which is not able to be whole", says the fire, "and therefore I devour seeking the absolute I do not find."[3]

When the Koala was stifled by smoke and heat, and the snake coiling itself around the foot of the sun had been singed, charred; . . . the moon came out.
It was the first death.
The moon turned black. She could not have kept her silvery shine with all the burnt out embers around her. Pulling the huge expanse of greyish-black cloth behind her, the moon figure extinguished the last remains of the fire and its victims.

Almost always there is silence, and there is silence now, and briefly the blend and stupefying moon eases the land of the torment of the drought.

The days are dry and hard, and the animals suffer.[4]

Violation against nature has taken place. The natural systems of the earth have been severed. Jagged and serrated outlines, part of movement structures were deeply etched in the space—a hand pointing upward; a torso tilting; arms, legs were twisted, bent or stiffened; extended lines of the body suddenly changed, shortened, angled. The direct movement connections had been broken. The spatial designs were those of cracklings, corrugations, shudderings. Are the inchoate forms on the floor, the tangle of limbs, the shapes of people? . . . burnt?

Deeply affected by the work of the author, Ivan Smith, and the artist, Clifton Pugh, in this classic piece of Australian Literature, I wanted to present the dramatic

[1] *The Dream Collector.* Arthur Tress. Westover Publishing Company, Virginia, 1972. A creative photographic record of the dreams and nightmares of the world of children.
[2] C.H.
[3] *The Bushfire.* Judith Wright. Angus and Robertson, 1979.
[4] *The Death of a Wombat.* Ivan Smith. Sun Books, Australia, 1979. This dance work is based on its theme and events. Performed in 1981 in the presence of Ivan Smith. Extract from the narrative.

narrative in such a way as to evoke the phenomena of nature and show its destructive power; the futile struggle for survival against this force of evil in nature (fire); the resistance by the native animals to the impending disaster; the plight of the animals caught in the raging fire in the drought-stricken Australian bush; the action of the heat of the sun on the glass, causing conflagration; the result of an act of human violation unleased against the bushland.

My group of thirty dance students reacted sensitively to the theme and through a series of improvisational experiences we began to crystallise details of movement and ways of moving. Our movement exploration was based on how animals move; shape, size and skin texture, habits, characteristics, qualities, instincts, range of movement, reaction to danger.

The bodies groped, prowled in mysterious shapes close to the floor; the long kinetic stretched out walks described the pacing stride of the dingo; what design of movement would express toughness? The broad sweeping movement of the kangaroo contrasted with the thumping jumps of contained rage and painful twistings of the limbs.

Find ways to walk or waddle as wombat. How does one confront an adversary? Experiment in space with walking or running patterns, weight transferences, balances.

Work with a partner in contrasting movement—timid—eager; small inward movements of parts of the body, in contrast to open, joyful feelings reflected in the spring, buoyancy and spontaneity of movement. Other movement contrasts could be aggressive—kick—strike with powerful oppositional movement, in contrast to fear with curled, weak, fluctuating body design, retreating steps; a prowling motif. Develop the awareness of counter tension as the hunter seeks the hunted.

How would one move when threatened by danger?

Observe an animal as it lies down, stands up, gathers food, attacks, defends. Convey the characteristics and quality of the movement.

Explore the awareness of an animal moving at night; see the world from upside down!

SUN-FIRE CHORUS

You will need to free the suffering of the earth and animals; the dust; the blazing steel rims of fiery destruction.

As you turn to each other, see the charred bodies of rocks; you are intimately concerned with the suffering of the remnants of this landscape; connect the tensions through the body; compression of energy to be released in explosive action.

The power of the sun and fire merge. The figures are densely packed together, accenting velocity, ruthlessness, brightness, heat, desiccation, burning.

Sense the dryness and dried-up-ness.

The work is composed in four movements:

bottles

dingo

kangaroo

wombat

A flux of movement . . . fire in the movement . . . it will cause pain and suffering . . .

The three protagonists, dingo, kangaroo and wombat stretch forward in a balance on the rostrum (symbol: ledge, rock), taut, alert. They are sensitive to the impending drama—in close proximity to each other—almost transparent—nerves, blood, muscles, torso, head, pelvis, back, feet, ears—silence. There are movement changes in slow motion giving an indication of the fearful tension.

Wombat is still frozen in a movement of lurching, ambulating—his four feet (hands and feet) are planted squarely and with a sense of awkwardness on the floor. The shape is heavy—knees bent, back rounded. He is shy, his instincts warn him of danger—he lifts one paw momentarily (foot).

Dingo, suspicious; head is turned sharply, followed by the torso—his line is horizontal—two-dimensional movement—he is both hunter and hunted. Tension throughout the body. The stance of the balance is parallel—archaic.

First Movement

A bottle lies here, brown, unbroken.

Before noon, more than twelve hundred square miles of bushland will be totally destroyed.[1]

It could be a bag or a cocoon—sheets of clear plastic are wrapped around two figures—the bottle shapes. They pull, tug, stretch, twist their plastic enclosure—we begin to see the changing outlines of this form and it is unsettling!

It is not a robot; it is going to encounter a force that will uproot and shatter its smooth exterior into myriads of fragments—like the fractional segments of broken ice.

The sun pours on to the bottle near the road.[2]

The sun-fire chorus begins a sequence of rhythmic dynamic movement, to approach the bottle shapes, who simultaneously release their own dimension of energy, within the framework of the plastic boundaries—the chorus linked by body contact move as one; a movement synthesis of sharp changes of level; bodies are supported one against the other; the energy and changing dimensions expand, extend, prolongate; there is an outpouring of more and more vigorous movement.

There are changing proportions of widely extended movement from within the plastic folds—surfaces are curvilinear, translucent hollows; inside are two figures interlocked, turning and twisting smoothly and spontaneously in contrast to the firm angular zigzag movements of the sun-fire chorus.

As the light catches the plastic material, it creates a dappled effect which by the end of the movement has turned to a blazing red!

All movement by the sun-fire group begins to accelerate—they separate and increase in force, speed, and range, circling the bottles, their movements flicker!

Spiralling and spinning in a series of quickly changing dynamics and directions the bottle shapes burst through their pliable mould . . . they fall into the fire; everything "billows and burns".

---

[1] *The Death of a Wombat.* Ivan Smith. Sun Books, Australia, 1979. Extract from the narrative.
[2] *Ibid.*

The Death of a Wombat
Photograph: Brian Bird

Snatching the plastic material the sun-fire group throw, curve, twist, wind and unwind the scorching edges.

A short, round thing of glass has woken the terror of the ages.[1]

and it is one long bellow of fire!?[2]

Second Movement

The dingo, cunning and unconquerable, unconquerable through his cunning, turns to watch the screaming dance of the approaching fire.[3]

His head is stretched forward, focus slightly down as if following a track; directional floor changes are rapid, the pattern is in circles; he travels by means of runs, trotting steps; the movement levels are low . . . furtive; economy of movement. His shape is two dimensional. Pulls of tension become linear extensions between all parts of the body.

Movement is spanned out into the space by the sun-fire chorus—they travel in turns and pivots in the four main directions, finishing in contraction—sit to the floor—this travelling (locomotion) pattern becomes a new floor design, creating the image of a whirlwind. They prepare to close off the dingo's escape route, forming a structure of narrow lines to become a maze.[4]

But the dingo cannot escape the demon of the approaching fire. In his flight he plunges through the opening created by the intricacy of the maze design.

He must race through the fire![5]

It is impossible to move outside this structure. Moving in one direction, the dingo discovers that the exit is blocked; he must find a new route; up and down, across and back—he runs, long and low, fast; he trots quickly across and back—rapid repetition—trapped!

The space between the route narrows—the dingo makes one more attempt to free himself. By springing upward and forward as if to propel himself far above the group who are converging upon him.

The dingo moves himself to his feet with the shouting flame two hundred yards away. He shakes himself briefly like a dog and then tilts back his head with the action of a wolf. He starts forward, moving easily to meet the fire. And as he moves, his body sinks lower and the paws work harder on the ground giving an athlete's rhythm . . . working harder . . . and then the long, lean head sits low, the body gathers speed with the powerful galloping action of the paws. Seconds before he meets the flames, the dingo reaches cheetah-speed. He plunges through them, eyes shut, head thrust down between the flashing forward legs.[6]

He falls!

[1] *The Death of a Wombat.* Ivan Smith. Sun Books, Australia, 1979. Extract from the narrative.
[2] *Ibid.*
[3] *Ibid.*
[4] Streets and Lanes. The group divides equally into lines. They all face one direction. On a given signal they make a quarter turn and face a new direction.
[5] *The Death of a Wombat.* Ivan Smith. Sun Books, Australia, 1979. Extract from the narrative.
[6] *Ibid.*

The Death of a Wombat
Photograph: Brian Bird

The group hold his limbs—they turn and twist him. Bending over him—they scrutinise!

Third Movement

> At first the kangaroo easily outpaced the fire. With a lope of forty miles in an hour he has kept the flames well behind him. The snakes and the koalas die, the dingos wait their chance, the kangaroo leaps on, and rests, and then takes up again his ancient choreography of limbs and head.[1]

A wall—a barrier—the group are tightly sealed.

The two kangaroos are breathing hard; their muscles contract ready to release them to freedom—the strong legs prepare to jump. They make their flying jumps in an orbital curve—they are met by the enemy.

This is the correlative—the kangaroos will try to make one more desperate attempt to break through this barricade of orange lights. The fire filled antagonists will interact, attempting to arrest the vertical and horizontal leaping.

They must outwit these innocent and courageous creatures; disorient them, shock, disinherit, injure; extinguish.

[1] *The Death of a Wombat.* Ivan Smith. Sun Books, Australia, 1979. Extract from the narrative.

The Death of a Wombat
Photograph: Brian Bird

The flames have trapped the flying kangaroos.[1]

The jumping "is almost at random now—this contest is unfairly matched—the protagonists summon all wisdom, all powers; they take off effortlessly and are tossed by the horde . . . and the flames feed".[2]

Fourth Movement

The chorus remain close together, in contact, as they interweave in a synthesis of rising and falling, bending, twisting, curling and uncurling, seething restlessness.

The bodies tense with savage and merciless vigour, the wombat limps unevenly into the centre. Everything now shifts wildly—short, sharp asymmetrical thrusts of arms and legs—the group dodges from place to place. The wombat falls, curls over, rolls, contracts with fear . . .

Because of his burns he can only take the weight on two or three of his body parts—limping he lumbers away searching for the river.

The furnace spreads then narrows following him. The wombat can be seen slowly travelling, allowing the movement to lead him to the next, laborious and awkward—but his slowness and clumsiness are a drawback . . . he cannot escape . . .

Like fireworks, the sun-fire group burst into swirling flame-like gyrating movement—they pass and re-pass the wombat, sweeping over him.

> He makes the miracle of reaching the river
> Slowly he slides under the water.[3]

As if driven by a new unpredictable force the group turn, change direction and with accelerated steps, runs, turns, move—move out of sight.

The disunity of lines, angles, surfaces; the sharp unshapely movement; sinking, drooping distortions; the figures who are left in the space are symbols of the pain, suffering and torment.

> When the sun sets, the thunder has gone.
> The moon comes up.[4]

The moon, trailing her black folds—embers—drifts through the smouldering scene; shudderings, corrugations.

DANCE NOTES

We had as a frame of reference the author's introductory notes:

> I wanted to synthesise certain groups of human characteristics, and to set these groups in contrast in order to say something about human success and failure.

> The wombat seemed to be friendly, stupid, innocent, slow—all characteristics that I was looking for in the main figure.

> I read through biologies of other outback animals and found all I wanted. The kangaroo—strong, tough, but too stupid to win through in a calamity.

[1] *The Death of a Wombat.* Ivan Smith. Sun Books, Australia, 1979. Extract from the narrative.
[2] *Ibid.*
[3] *Ibid.*
[4] *Ibid.*

The koala—decent enough, but unimaginative and unenterprising, among the first types to go under in country-wide adversity. The dingo—tough, resilient, and with the cunning that sees people through when times are out of joint.

The wombat—with that sort of gentleness and vulnerability that make nice guys finish last.

My reading led me to think that a bushfire would provide a suitable social disaster common to the fates of these animal symbols.

Our senses and emotions had been awakened and we wanted to tell the story. The essence of the movement whether stationary or in travelling, was to evoke the images through stylized movement and to identify with the types of animals, their characteristic qualities and their plight; to be aware that this destructive force is present in our society; to retain the impact of the suffering; to create an experience which had potential to arouse awareness and compassion.

The large SUN-FIRE group worked creatively to build their structure for the group design, rhythmic connections in travelling and changing the possibilities of dynamics in the context of the thematic material in each section.

The compositional form evolved from the continuous process of improvisation. To further define the movement of the dingo, kangaroo, wombat, snake, I introduced a study of planal design; opposition, asymmetry—a return to the tensions of the archaic[1] aiming for the essential in movement.

We had to take into account the different individual rhythms and bodily skills, integrating them into a compact group shape for movement organisation and as a physical force, supporting the impact of each dramatic experience.

The writing was so powerful that I felt a musical score would blunt the impact. Instead I chose the plaintive sounds of the didgeridoo; and to link the events with crucial emotional responses, passages selected from the dramatic text, were spoken to accentuate suspense, horror, tenderness, defeat.

From the earliest times the moon and the sun have become symbols of the sacred myth of creation. "The sun, the symbol of the succession of life and death",[1] The moon is changing, appearing and reappearing—"female, symbol of fertility, vegetation and that life was always born anew"[2]—dark and light. "All dance, being imitative, aims at achieving identify with the thing observed and danced out. It is and gives ecstasy by virtue of being in touch with the life-force."[3]

SONG OF THE JUMBLIES

Far and few, far and few
Are the lands where the Jumblies live;
Their heads are green, and their hands are blue
And they went to sea in a Sieve.[4]

Inside everyone of us are tendencies that are similar to animals.[5]

[1] *The Sacred Dance.* Maria-Gabriele Wosien. Avon Books, New York, 1974.
[2] *Ibid.*
[3] *Ibid.*
[4] *The Jumblies—Nonsense Songs and Laughable Lyrics.* Edward Lear. Peter Pauper Press, Mount Vernon, New York, 1962. Music—The Bermuda Triangle—Tomita.
[5] *The Magic of Pictures. Enchanted World.* Byron Holme. Thames and Hudson, London, 1979.

After years of tantalizing glimpses of the nonsense poetry of Edward Lear I asked my students if they would be interested in the theme of The Jumblies for a new dance composition. They listened with delight to the humorous and curious expressions of his imagination in verse ... we found ourselves in the world of those eccentric creatures ... of fantastic body shapes and dress, unpredictable adventures and amusements, curious colours, tastes, frailties, habits, movements, surroundings; was there a parallel in this enchanging nonsense between certain aspects of the human being and characteristics of animals?

I thought of Merlin the Magician on his visits to his old friend King Arthur, instructing him on show to cope with all the pain, defeat and disillusionment that he had suffered during his personal relationships throughout his reign.

> "Unless," Merlin told Arthur, "you had lived this, you would not have known it. One has to live one's knowledge."[1]

The necromancer, in his wisdom, continues to suggest to Arthur that he should retire for a while to experience nature and observe the way in which the animal kingdom lives and survives. Thus, he will be able to acquaint himself with their political ideologies[2] and by so doing learn more effective ways of standing up to the disloyalty, deceit, rivalry and jealousy which has broken out among his family and The Knights of The Round Table.[2]

> "You are wanting me to find something out by learning from the beasts?", queries the King.[3]

Arthur listens intently to the prudence and far-sighteddness of his former tutor, as Merlin confides in him that for his education, he must become an ant,[4] and be transformed on later occasions into a bird, fish, badger and hedgehog. Increasing his understanding of the workings of the social and political order, would forestall unhappiness and discontent in the future. King Arthur is ready and willing to be "magicked".

> and Merlyn had taught him about animals, so that the single species might learn by looking at the problems of the thousands. He remembered the belligerent ants, who claimed their boundaries, and the pacific geese, who did not.[5]

Is there a lesson for us to be learnt as we mingle and mix with the Lear characters? Can we enliven our lives by wandering with their ebullient spirits?

Let us project ourselves into the affections and moods of the Jumblie population—the ways of their songs and steps, fun and jollity thus assembling our own version in dance.

We do not know where they originated. They do not seem to be sea creatures; nor do they burrow underground. Perhaps they are part of the fauna of the mountains. Are

[1] *The Book of Merlyn. The unpublished conclusion to the once and Future King.* T. H. White. University of Texas Press, 1977. Fontana—Collins, 1978, p. 3.
[2] *Ibid.*, p. 27.
[3] *Ibid.*, p. 81.
[4] *Ibid.*, p. 23.
[5] *The Once and Future King.* T. H. White. Dell Publishing Co., New York, 1960, p. 638.

they animal spirits, covered with fur or shells? They seem to have strange feet and almost no toes, or at least, they hide these features by scrunching or curling them up tightly—this gives an awkward and graceless rhythm to their walks. When this happy breed wish to swagger and exaggerate, they can let down a third leg[1]—this can be used to beat time (for they love to sing). It can also be waved about as a tail or used for the playing of games. When they are excited or frightened their legs tremble. They fall over a lot, but never hurt themselves; and "can dance in circlets all night long".[2]

Most of their movement is small, quick, dissonant and distorted—it is punctuated by pauses, changes of accent and rhythms which change in unpredictable ways, expressing an element of capriciousness and readiness to tease!

their heads are green, and their hands are blue.[3]

The eating habits of the Jumblies are somewhat unusual. Colours stream down from the sky like stalactites. They nibble, munch or lick their favourite colour which spirals, frills or ruffles above their heads. Golden yellow makes them feel healthy; after nibbling pistacio green they scream with laughter and dance all night; the greedy ones gobble up the striped colour treats—that can make a Jumblie quite bilious. "Colours" must be left behind when they set out on an adventure.

Like some of their dear friends, Pobble, The Dong, Mr Quangle Wangle Quee,[4] we decided to travel with the Jumblies to a far off land, far from hurry, worry and strife, and free from responsibility and care.

Our space is the great Gromboolian Plain[5]—pink and grey cloth covers part of the floor, masses of stretched deep blue material to be used as a boat, lies close by.

So, too are the Jumblie creatures, or ... almost ... they have just finished licking their favourite colour, lilac, which always makes them sway and grow dizzy and fall down. Some took the weight on two or three different parts of their body and rested—they never entirely relax into sleep—they are always restless and ready to start the next adventure! Heads move from side to side. While lying on the floor legs are raised, feet cross and tap each other, they like to rock or swivel on different parts of their bodies; it wakes them up! It is time for a little conversation—and communication—they engage in an absurd kind of rigmarole, isolating wrists, hips, shoulders, and other parts of the body, agreeing to some ideas, dissenting from others.

Tonia, one of the Jumblie girls (nine special dance students in the group), crouched low and executed an ingenious means of moving across the floor—she held one ankle firmly and changing weight forward, she dragged her leg behind, moving forwards or sideways. her feet were always flexed or toes curled up.

You could tell that some were engaged in friendly conversation while others grumbled—but all unwound from their resting positions to travel together to another part of the space—to the play ground.

So the pleasure-seeking Jumblies travelled fast and travelled light. Their colour

---

[1] The physical changes could reflect an inward change.

[2] *Nonsense songs and Laughable Lyrics*. Edward Lear. Peter Pauper Press, Mount Vernon, New York, 1962, p. 43.

[3] Edward Lear, Characters and Country.

[4] *Ibid*.

[5] *Ibid*.

The Jumblies
Photographs: Brian Bird

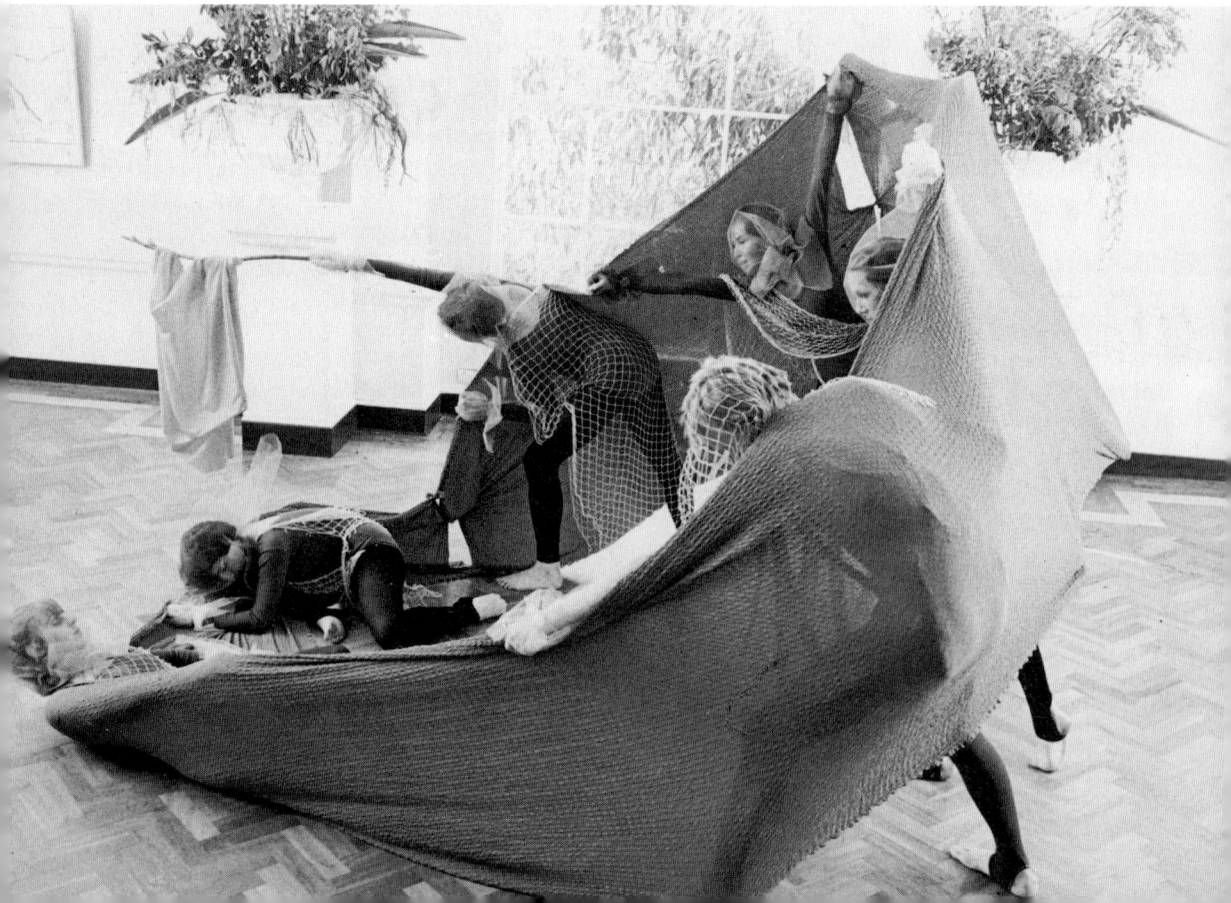

feasting habits were left at home on the plain; wish to escape from routine and convention, we fled with them.

We travelled with quick little steps—crossing one foot over in front and then behind; turning like sparklers with flicks of the foot and balanced momentarily. One by one we "followed the leader" who usually guided us in a serpentine pattern, until we reached the play ground. Then we ran and leapt to the music of Dominico Scarlatti (the Jumblies favourite composer). The colourful music gave us a feeling of motion, especially movement for the hands and body.

The Jumblie group now divided into twos and threes, each pair trying to outdo the other in acts and movements of bravado—acrobatic tricks, leap-frog, handstands, cartwheels; like old vaudeville performers they dashed through can-can steps and indulged themselves in horse-play and spontaneous unpredictable stunts and games. Finally they formed a chain in which the whole group became twisted and tumbled about in their unpredictable world. The little fun-loving tricksters were good-natured and had another amusing idea. They stomped away and returned with gigantic silver goblets.[1]

They adopted attitudes, mannerisms, movements and even accents (voice) of the aristocracy; holding their goblets in an exaggerated manner they walked about the space in the most elegant style—the body swayed slightly back and the hips were thrust forward, stopping only to posture or occasionally falling sideways. The walks became more sensuous, the pelvic movements more accentuated; provocative!

Raising the goblets to their lips they drank and chanted—"Ha! — Ha! — Ha!" These sounds were made at different times in different pitches and resonances and always with great liveliness. At the end of the party the goblets were thrown away with a grand gesture. An element of decorum changed the scene; the Jumblies restrained their movement; no more grandiose gestures or irresponsible laughter. They displayed an underlying gentility as they changed their movement style to suit the other eccentric folk of the world of Lear; small delicate runs and springs as one Jumblie attempted to catch a butterfly; she barely touched the ground. Two figures made a turtle shape on the floor (on the knees, flat back, outstretched arms). They moved about slowly with the figure of the Pobble seated on their back, enjoying the ride! The graceful lady Jingly-Jones[2] formed her arms or legs into the shape of a mallet and made small hitting strokes, as in the game of croquet. Other Jumblies played at shuttlecock and battledore. The sequence was for four players—imaginary bats were held, making forehand or backhand strokes—the hand or foot was often thrust out as if to stop the ball—long lunges were executed in different directions in the course of the game—all movement and gesture was in a slow motion.

The leader of the Jumblies changed the mood and the pace. A signal from her, and the group opened the blue fabric which was stretched, extended and spread into changing shapes. The nine figures enfolded themselves in the pliable sheath-like mould. A simple movement plan evolved, as nine dancers were now moving as one. They lifted, threw, moved it up and down, round and round—this manipulation of the material expressed the plunging waves, while bending, stretching and running movements by the figures inside the frame of material, created the image of a boat tossing in the water. One side of the floating shape was lifted as the other side sank downwards or lowered.

[1] Goblets were made of papier-mache and silver paper.
[2] Edward Lear, Characters and Country.

The constant changing swirls and sweep of the circling lines depended on the guidance, pressure and weight exerted by the Jumblie group. In the last phrase of the ebb and flow of the movement of currents, the fabric was thrown high into the air until it billowed. As it descended, the shape contracted sinking to the floor, covering the Jumblies. Like the tide washing over shells and rocks, the crouching figures moved along underneath it, searching on the sandy floor of the ocean for a new adventure singing their refrain:

> Far and few, far and few
> Are the lands where the Jumblies live;
> their heads are green, and their hands are blue
> And they went to sea in a sieve.

In our eagerness to join the exploits of this band of happy-go-lucky absurd characters, we had ignored our sense of safety, duty and responsibility, so endangering the lives of ourselves and others.

In that instant when the boat collapsed and we contracted to the floor, sucked down, submerged, did the realisation manifest itself, that we had been sailing in . . . a sieve!

SONG OF THE JUMBLIES—a creative composition for children[1]

My friends the Jumblies, could hardly contain their joy at finding they were going to be re-created . . . they were going to mingle once more with the real world. They loved the young and the very old; . . . humans who believed in fantasy. Now they were to be re-awakened by children, who would share in their way of life . . .

> In the past they could frolic and bound about all day, and "at night by the light of the Mulberry Moon, they danced to the flute of the Blue Baboon".[2]

> Would the children join The Jumblies in their sweet eating habits?

> Would they all set out in a sieve for erratic adventures in a far-off land?

Since a composition is a related coherent combination of movement, it is better to use the movement sparingly, each movement evolving out of the other.

If one sequence of movement is created it can then be arranged in different ways; positioning of bodies, heights, speeds, angles, directions.

Narrow or widen your movements. Choose a simple movement theme expressing the special group character of frivolity—travel to your playground for prankish games; spiral like a star; become a snail; explosions; quickened crescendo!

The children made a house of twigs, magic, and royal blue smiles . . . a bird's wing flew . . . a sail . . .

There was preoccupation as they struggled to bring the world of fantasy into objective reality and create a shape that would move, sail, float, toss, capsize, drift, dip, sway.

---

[1] Grade Seven; eleven and twelve years of age. Weekly visits for one term to Marist College, Woolwich; 1985, recreating part of the choreography of Jumblies. (Teacher, Jan Bush (Daly), a former dance student of mine, C.C.E. Castle Hill Campus, Sydney.)

[2] "Quangle Wangle's Hat". *Nonsense Songs and Laughable Lyrics*. Edward Lear. Peter Pauper Press, New York, 1962.

We need to develop the process, devising ways and means by which we could sail away in our sieve, adding contrast to the inconsequential antics of the fun-loving unique characters.

I believe in the words of D. H. Lawrence who calls it "enkindled awareness"; the way in which the power of the imagination can bring a child into the state of being fully alive.

Some groups travelled in unison—limbs quivered—arm strokes were swift and sharp; designs of structures melted . . . disappearing foam; shapes flowed with the tide of the breath.

Each group created their imaginary sea-scapes with plasticity and energy; spiralling as in a whirlpool; drifting, rising falling, bent or stretched, closed or opened; figures crouching and running in circles within stretched material—sheath-like—swirling heaving currents; a figure ran with the sail, the banner, flaunting!

Few of the class could fail to be enchanted by the whimsical and satirical qualities in the verse of Edward Lear. I modified the choreography to suit the level of dance ability of the young students, dividing them into groups, approximately six or seven girls in each group. We were ready to try out the possibilities for dance invention so that the members of the class would have an insight into the process of creating.

The movements of strange design were simplified. Yet, it was not merely a matter of changing a symmetrical line with one small movement, such as turning the foot up into flexed position, or the head tilting off-centre; but a concentrated effort by the class to understand and be aware of the physical pulls from one part of the body leading into the next—extending further into unpredictable lines; nothing resolved harmoniously; an increased consciousness in the planes of the body, as one part opposed the other; one hip turned in against the opposite knee; both arms twisting, reaching in the opposite direction to that hip which is thrust out; the inward tensions; balances on different parts of the body as one attained the dissonance of the incongruities; expressing elements of idiosyncrasy and eccentricity present in the Jumblie characters.

"Develop your awareness for communication! Go beyond words and express your feelings through movements, conveyed by the interconnection of strange designs."

In the next segment, pause to look at the floor patterns you are making, while travelling. Circles, zig-zagging, diagonals; the groups form; the movement is quick, light, springy, interspersed with turns and small jumps; a twist of part of the body, a limb; focus on inventive possibilities; travelling at a low level.

Be aware of the arrangement of bodies in the composition. The class of thirty-six to forty students used the space to explore and innovate, discovering the self and others.

The Jumblies love the impermanence of change; to re-unite and separate, scatter; they move in peculiar ways; are contradictory; so the moving structures of each group in the class were diverse; shapes shifted; opposite pulls between bodies stretched the movement lines taught—a frame:

For instance, if there are seven figures in a group, place one at either end, three plus two at different levels and spaces, within the structure; if there are four figures in a design place three in a triangle and one asymmetrically.

Your travelling is small-scale, the space being filled with groups moving; fit the dimensions of your arrangement into the space available. You will need an insight into the ways of the Jumblies. Moods, movements, signals; they need to become a part of *your* mind and imagination.

Are the foibles of The Jumblies, the disparate characteristics of our own selves?

Illusions

COLLAGE IN DANCE AND SOUND

I wanted to work within a sound collage putting together ideas from disparate sources, which would emerge as a group of images in dance, suited to the medium of collage, expressing its own imaginative life. To create an open space for the dancer's own thoughts and feelings in which to wander. To travel into other perceptions, images and memories conveyed by the colours and textures of the sound.

From what vantage point will we enter the dimensions of the sound collage?

By approaching the sound in an oblique way movement would be juxtaposed against the shrill tonal clusters; the flat two-dimensional space changes to a deeper three-dimensional space by the presence of a central image around which other images can cling.

Like the sound, the movement continuities change, shift and dissolve. Movement endings become blurred, indirect, indefinite. all the levels of sound movement relationships, themes, images are interchangeable. They may re-appear somewhere else, or melt into imaginative kinaesthetic experiences between the dancers.

What strange and adventurous chords are evoked in us as we proceed towards the vastness of the uninhabited sound space.

Generating the movement dialogue is improvisation, while the creative patterns of the shapes are contrasted and transformed by imagination into thematic narrative or an abstract version.

Assemble, link, superimpose layers of images already stored from experience, observation, dream, memory. Reflect, remember. Do not slide along the superficial layer of yourself!

The range of imagery can be unrelated or seemingly inappropriate, often surreal. Movement and meaning can be disrupted, displaced by a surprise reaction to a sound, an impulse, object, or a chance intermingling of movement images.

The dance themes can exist quite independently from the complex array of sound. One can proceed in quite another direction ... to other solutions. Recall images from former compositions and alter, re-locate them in a new expressive reality.

In the context of the overlapping of movement and imagery there needs to be a focus and a disclosure of meaning. Collage may have the inconsistencies of the dream, but the material has to be shaped, revealing an imagination at work, creating the surprise of new movement relationships.

Allow the collage to grow, link your images. It is a rich medium to work in; there is always something to find out. One is drawn into a curious perception and awareness, which keeps deepening, as the meaning of the thematic sequences unfold.

In practise, the sequence order in the composition may be changed; endings incomplete; movements suspended or spontaneously taken up again and changed; images fragmented to assume different forms of expression.

ILLUSIONS

COLLAGE IN DANCE AND SOUND

This collective or mosaic of unrelated ideas, images and elements became the centre of a dance experience with students of The Sydney Dance Development Centre,[1] over a period of eight weeks in 1989.

The stimulus for the creative sessions was the treatment of the theme of collage. Each fragment brought its own qualities to the layering of ideas in the variations of movement, assuming different characteristics, yet part of the whole thematic material.

Movement shifts, chance encounters, emotional changes, patterns in a given span of time were utilized in the stream of images corresponding to tenderness, flaws (shadows), non-relatedness, the tensions and restlessness of the group movement.

At first the levels of creative development and imaginative thinking within the group varied; increased understanding of the textures, kinetic quality and flow of energy in the collage heightened the sense of awareness and unity amongst the dancers.

We established a growing confidence in the availability of body movements for the physical expressiveness and the shape and timing of the movement connections in this diverse material.

The following descriptions are of the fragmented narratives which maintain as a central core, the quality of tenderness.

In the final installation another possibility is available to the group. They will be able to make the decision as to the choice of material in the process of "cut-up"; editing and cutting up of any part of the movement information; re-ordering or adding to the collage in another way, which should be economical, interesting and hold one's attention.

Fragment 1

The dance figures are placed one behind the other in a diagonal line. Lunging to the same side, arms are extended sideways. Every second individual now changes the position of the lunge and turns to the opposite side.

The movement level changes from the lunge to a wide deep fall to the floor. The symmetrical design is altered and the floor design becomes an oval shape. The dancers assume the curved design of fish ... going up and coming down; there is a certain uniformity in the abstract relationship of the figures, different from the unfamiliar characteristics of collage—there is tension in the design, contrast and symmetry in the relationship.

[1] Dance students of The Diploma in Dance Education. A private tertiary college course, accommodated at Kuringai College of Advanced Education, Sydney, Director, Ann Butt.

Fragment 2

The dancers are juxtaposed against a wall. They represent the flaws, shadows, weaknesses or fears, which a young girl believes are the expressions of her interior life. Their strange shape gives them a dramatic presence.

The shape definition is an image of "hanging"—necks are relaxed, heads droop downwards, back or sideways with a feeling of weight. One arm hangs limply, the other is stretched upwards. The bodies oscillate. The figures are enmeshed in their contradictions.

Wishing to rid herself of the inadequacies in her human psyche the girl struggles to transfer them to some external surface—in this instance she chooses the wall. They hang as if stapled. Running to the adjacent wall she tilts against it and watches the inverted, asymmetrical movements of this enchained group. The figures explore the possibilities of using the wall as a source for the exploration of movement. The turned inwardness of the body shapes mirrors the emotional distortion of the "flaws". the young girl pulls them away from the wall; these dissonant figures edge closer together.

Fragment 3

The figures pursue one another across the space in an attempt to rid themselves and each other of the images which twist and divide them.

The group move at random with runs and triplets; they confront each other, while executing off-centre leg extensions. Breaking away they present a statement of rejection in the shape of non-related juxtaposed angles of movement; they move away from each other in side lunges, torso and side contractions. Deliberate walks lead them into a new space.

Illusions
Photograph: Branco Gaica

Sound of the collage musical composition intrudes; clipped and metallic, introducing an echo of a childhood memory. A figure skips across the space with single and double steps. The group Chant ... "my mother said, that I never should, play with the gypsies in the wood" ... a crescendo of fast skipping.

I run to greet my mother in the room with green and gold lace curtains and "pearls for tears".

Fragment 4

A leaf of grass. Couples and small groups were sitting on the grass. It was a fragment of life in the park.

They sat side by side, legs were bent or stretched. The lines of human movement shifted imperceptibly as the body weight and its direction changed.

Settling into their respective positions some created a sense of rest and relaxation, reclining on one or both elbows; heads inclined.

The body design changed to symmetry and legs bent and arms folded around the knees.

Sitting upright, legs extended to parallels. Half awake, half asleep, the group watched the people hurrying by. From a group of three figures sitting side by side in unison, one moved to form a triangle; the straight line was broken; the third figure defined asymmetrically.

Unexpectedly, one in a group of four, stood up and moved to another part of the space.

Others changed their level by lying down on the grass area, one arm flung sideways. Serene in the sunlight, the mood was tranquil; everything was uncomplicated. The formal design of figures in the park appeared to have been pre-arranged.

The space expanded. Couples stood up, loitered, walked or ran down the slope, disappearing into the crowd.

> her ringlets fell upon the page
> she held up the title
> "Illusions"?

Fragment 5

> "Touching and melting
>
> Nowhere" [1]

Drifting together two people convey an expression of tenderness. Curved lines of movement create the intimacy, the link between the figures. The nearness of each one to the other introduces a means of communicating the awareness of rediscovery.

Facing, they bend in deep plié from either first or second position; their aims are lightly entwined. The pelvis contracts, and the couple effortlessly descend to the floor—they sit one behind the other, facing the same direction. There is a breath connection as the bodies bend forward and back. Arms open and close, enfolding. The legs, slightly bent, in second position.

Through the physical contact and weight distribution the forms intermingle. The facility of movement allows them to bend, twist, and achieve a continuity of a dance

[1] *Ariel Poems*. Sylvia Plath. Faber and Faber, London, 1965.

Illusions
Photograph: Branco Gaica

phrase. They extend this continuity in standing. In their movement images they spin out the fragility of tenderness; the back breathes against that of the partner; an arm is outstretched across a thigh; the neck circles against a hand; in a lift the body mirrors the line of the partner's body. In the flow of movement in this duet there is little separation. Walt Whitman sings in his poems of the delight in the body and its physical movement.

The expressive images unfold in complementary spirals, in a spirit of simplicity and beauty. The couple remain in a small frame in the space joined in an embrace.

Fragment 6

At the same time the group engage in their transcient relationships. The interludes are brief. There is the suggestion of the feeling of tenderness, but it is short-lived, fragmented. The fractional element underlies the group interchange of contact. Centres of balance shift, and the mood fluctuates. The movement dissolves, the couples turn away.

In search of their forgotten selves, the figures seek new possibilities in the changing relationships. Moves are stretched out across the space. There is a burst of dynamic energy; the feeling of tenderness is overwhelmed by the sharp, abrupt, ominous movement of their aggressive instincts. Each one moves forward and back in an energy flow, changing direction, involved in speeding up the attack. Momentarily, parts of the body, foot, back, shoulder, knee, become the focus of the contact.

The stable point in the space is the organic phrasing of movement in the tender duet.[1]

Fragment 7

A new character appears carrying a bouquet of red flowers. This is the bride and groom, symbolizing the dual aspects in our nature.

In syncopated tango-like walks, it glides across the space. Quick changes of rhythmic steps, sharp and staccato isolations of body movement express a lively mood. The figure tosses the bouquet into the air and the group scramble to catch this symbol of happiness! Chanting and swaying they tear at the petals ... "loves me ... loves me not ... loves me ... not ..."

At first the movements towards each other were gentle, protective; a tender expression; gestures dissolve into "Touching and melting, Nowhere".

"Loves me not" has awakened their fears. All lightness has changed into lines and accents which are hard and stilted. They communicate a feeling of aggression in jerky thrusts of the hips. The tender feelings have disappeared. Moving hypnotically the cluster becomes a tightly moving mass; from an open space to a closed space; the high-pitched wail of sound penetrates the wedge and a figure falls to the floor, rolling out of focus. There is little life or movement ... negative silence.

Fragment 8

The bride and groom traces a circle around the couple as if to protect the gently developing nature of their feelings. There is a change in the sometimes playful and jesting character. It becomes introspective, alone, receding into a corner. Sliding into wide, wild lunges the body changes into twisted inversions and falls clumsily against the wall, into a knotted shape. It expresses a precarious and vulnerable image.

Fragment 9

Combining oval lines and shapes, the contours of movement of parts of the body, connect the closeness of feeling in the duet. Supportive gestures attach the figures. In quiet phrases of movement the girl arches back out of the shape of the male. One enfolds the other, creating a unity of an expression of tenderness.

We completed the idea of collage with the device of "cut-up".

To find new combinations of the fragments of the composition which could provide a different order, a new meaning. We made our own choices while experimenting with the process of "cut-up".

Each fragment was numbered with the descriptions of the movement theme or sequence and recorded on separate cards. The dancers had a number within the nine

[1] Meghan Hoffman, Sam Emmans; Freelance Dance Company; Sydney Dance Development Centre.

Illusions
Photograph: Branco Gaica

segments; each chose a card at random. For instance, in the overall structure of each experiment there was a complete re-ordering of fragmented material; a succession of changes, beginning and ending with the different movements and images.

Each section can be fragmented into even smaller segments, so that the juxtaposition and proportion of "found material" is accentuated. The impression of truth in the collage, in this composition, the quality of tenderness, is almost hidden in the stream of changing movement fragments.

DANCE NOTES

While the principles of collage have been for a long time acknowledged in virtually every field of the arts during the 1980s, there have been some interesting developments in the use of collage in underground experimental music and related arts which have gone virtually undocumented save for a few articles in ephemereal publications. It seems that there are a growing number of individuals in this post-industrial society in the world, often isolated geographically, who through the mail allow this music to survive and has indeed formed part of its aesthetic.[1]

Interested in the musical activities of these creative people, I discovered sound collages which could be a possible source for a process in dance.

The organization of the musical sounds is in a most concentrated form, mixing raw sound material on tape from a wide range of sources by individual artists and structured into a collage form; "a hetereogeneous mixture produced a highly animated mosaic of composition with an engaging mixture of recognizable and unrecognizable sounds".[2]

Collage has often been associated with disruption; the peculiarities of irrational juxtaposition and collisions between sounds, all part of the underlying principles in the complex layering of the processes.

The fragmentation or cut-up of the sound structures, dynamics, rhythms, spaces, distances, silences and tensions are part of a stream of "split-second sound fragments".[3] The multiplicity of images dissolve, evaporate like the endings of a dream.

Whether the expressive energies of the sound composition is written for tape recorder, electronic means, "found-sound" or conventional techniques, the musical content is animated by unpredictability, unexpectedness, inappropriateness. This serves to animate a score for dance collage.

One has the freedom of choice to relate and coincide with the sound combinations, or form one's own dance references, movement and ideas, forming alternative and independent possibilities.

Impressions at first can be chaotic because of the unfamiliarity of the sounds and the relationships; one must absorb them through the ear and into one's consciousness, if one is to accept the activity as an imaginative source.

The contemporary concrète music can be lighthearted, humourous, violent, chaotic, irrational, vibrating with life; a disguise of the real meaning changed by personal fantasy. It supports contradictory ideas.

The sound elements in La Ronde by Michael Chion,[4] showed indications of expressivity that could be applied to the untitled fragments of this movement collage S.B.O.T.H.I. P16 D4[5] augmented the torn movement surfaces with exclamations of stridency, sonorous discord, acute and piercing, coming to an end, as the group quivered with density, severing the quality of tenderness.

The figure of the "bride and groom"[6] was inspired by the photographic image, created by Arthur Tress; based on the unification of male and female impulses in the psyche (Jung).

In the phrase of group movement aligned in symmetrical design, the vitality is less, but the impact is through repetition. There is a feeling of order, composure. The motif is often the symmetrical designs by the artist, M. C. Escher who believed in the positive and negative effects in art; of contrasting relationships in symmetry and repetition. One can also conceptualize this in movement through the mirror image.

[1] "Collage and Noise". Jon Walker. *Art and Australia*, Vol. 26.
[2] *Ibid.*, No. 1, Spring 1988. Correspondence with Jon Walker, 1988–89.
[3] *Ibid.*
[4] La Ronde. Michael Chion, Composer. France.
[5] S.B.O.T.H.I. P16 D4, Composers. West Germany.
[6] *Talisman*. Arthur Tress. Thames and Hudson, New York, 1986.

Two Metaphoric Approaches

THE OYSTER GLIDE

Addressing the problem of the pollution of oysters in the Georges River, Sydney.

A personal analogy in dance and words; making the familiar strange. A hinge for communication.

Creativity Workshop 1989. Centre for Human Aspects of Science and Technology, the University of Sydney.

They raved about "The Palais Glide", but it was nothing compared to the sensational "Oyster Glide"!

We would promenade up and down, a slow turn, then skim around the corners opening into a balance that was longlasting. Free and supple we would often risk a new rhythmic freedom while trying out a step. our shape undulated like the edge of a flower.

The oyster-grey sheath-like dresses clung to our skin, which under the light appeared translucent; our smooth exterior seemed to move and shift. We smiled with the applause. Teasing the admirers, we retreated into our capes as if into a shell. They tried to touch and hold us, saying that "we looked good enough to eat!"

The group kept close together and danced in pairs, gliding to and fro; we felt as though we were floating.

Clinging to each other we sped around the floor, performing "Oyster Loops"— an intricate movement ornamentation of curves and arcs with changes of weight. The space exploded with spiralling jumps. "The Posh ladies" compared our style with that of The Lobster Quadrille, but if Lewis Carroll had seen "The Oyster Glide" he would have commanded us to teach a variation of the slippery walk to Alice, the Gryphon and the Mock Turtle.

Some said that it was the "impurities"—minute irritations in the air that changed us. We became vague and troubled and no longer floated free and pure. The colour of our skin faded, dark blotches spreading over the delicate surfaces. The oyster grey dresses began to shrink, scarcely covering us. No longer tranquil, we could not change our shape fluently; faces began to wrinkle and lose their pearl-like quality. All movement stiffened. Spectators tried to prize us apart, but the group solidified into a mass. (Some years later the dancers of "The Oyster Glide" were discovered preserved in a wall of ice.)

Straying from my partner, I climbed to the top of a staircase and sheltered in a small room.

I sit here, hardly moving, a victim of these invisible disorders. I do not go out. I feel as if I am locked in a shell.

People walk past my room. they say "never see her, you know, close as an oyster"—but I don't care. I dream of the days, when, with hair flying and the spirit alight with the fire of the dance, we would face each other and perform the fluent rhythms of "The Glide"; and when in my imagination I hear the mysterious watery sounds of the music . . . I sway.

INSECTA VIRILITAS

Addressing the problem of an insect located in a space station.

A personal analogy in dance and words; making the familiar strange. A hinge for communication.

Creativity Workshop 1989. Centre for Human Aspects of Science and Technology, the University of Sydney.

On waking up, I unfolded my wings, opened the feelers or antennae locked in sections of my body, then stretched the spine and limbs, which were like the strings of a violin. Extending two protruberances from the side of the head, I listened to messages given by the team of scientists; they were preparing us for a special mission into space. We were to be the first insect colony to live in "the floating gardens"; mounds of flowers and plants which use colour and pattern for insect camouflage and metamorphosis; I looked forward to these transformations somewhere in space and time.

The daily routine began with bending, stretching and twisting the segments; accenting the mobility of joints and hinges by executing movements of isolation of the body and its parts. We could move one part of our body quite separately from another part. The increased movement gave us growth and energy to walk, run, jump, paddle, crawl, roll and fly.

To keep ourselves alive we may have to leap across a crater or follow the course of a stream of coloured liquid. One could press a spot on one's body and an antenna would emerge; it was a hearing organ and used to transmit sound; it also acted as a trumpet when we wished to play music.

At the end of our legs were minute pads which took the weight when landing from a jump; after flexing and pointing these narrow extremities, we would rise on the points and running very fast to receive vibrations, open our wings and fly!

If we wished to rest the scientists encouraged us to sit or kneel and to practise eye and head movements such as rotating, lifting and dropping, responding to changes in the light intensity. Our vision was extremely sensitive and we could navigate better in the dark.

By moving sideways in long, low jumps, we could cluster into groups, communicating with one another with the liveliness of crickets.

A panorama of stars flashed across a screen in the laboratory. Drumming our bodies against each other, we beat with the points of our feet and wings against the moving parade—as if to bombard our enemies or rivals!

In order to prepare to forage for food, the two front feelers were locked together and as we clambered along, we made sharp digging and pushing thrusts in our search for particles of food.

I remember one experiment with weightlessness. We were all herded into the anti-gravity module—astronauts and insects alike—we amused every one with our acrobatic feats of agility as we hung by one feeler or ran with crossed legs across the surface of the ceiling. The astronauts floated clumsily, bumping their strange armour in a ritualistic space dance.

At the end of our training we could roll along erratic paths as if avoiding obstacles, suspend in mid-air and control our balance while pulsating.

We will soon be leaving Planet Earth to inhabit a glowing new world. In the preparation for take-off, our wings were folded, the limbs tied and eyes pushed neatly back into the head. We were then poured into a membranous sac and stored in the space ship.

The spider intervened. He could not spin a perfect web in the island in space—in *that* shifting atmosphere—and refusing to travel, curled up and went to sleep.

For decades Insecta Virilitas have lived in "the floating gardens", diving into amethyst stems of plants, chatting under half-submerged flowers, seeking out in caves the whims of their invisible world.

Children's Dance

CHILDREN DANCING ...
CHILDREN CREATING

> The presence of the young lightens the world and changes it from an oppressive, definitive, solidified one to a fluid, potentially marvellous, malleable, variable, as yet to be created world. I call them the transparent children ... and I return to my transparent world, where the young say spontaneous things, act by their dreams, seek their fantasies to be fulfilled.[1]

I found a conducive atmosphere with children of grade four, dancing and creating with their class-room teacher, John Caradia. He established a lively interest in working creatively, involving himself and the class in the love of movement.[2]

Here was an opportunity for me to work again with the child in dance; to experience their wonder, imagination and vitality. To be free from pressure to conform to the stereotype. This meant that we would adopt a flexible open-minded approach, we could be adventurous. We could explore anywhere or anything imaginable. We could be adventurous, interpreting the adventures, imaginings and pretendings, in a way through movement, that would increase sensitivities, abilities and needs.

By continuing the sense of awareness of the body as an instrument of expression, the possibilities of ways of moving could be increased; each child exploring their physical emotional, imaginative world, forming their creative expressions with others.

It was an exhilarating process with the weekly dance sessions continuing throughout the year,[3] during which time the children's talents were developed (both boys' and girls'). Their lively interest in thinking, feeling, moving, needed recognising, shaping, directing, so that they could begin to organize their own creative efforts. To receive the benefits of working in the creative materials of dance, in movement and imagination suggestions were made by John and myself as to how they could transform the physical movement into creative expression.

---

[1] *The Journals of Anais Nin.* Volume Four. Quartet Books, London, 1974.

[2] Grade four, boys and girls, average age 10 years. St Joseph's Primary School, Moorebank, N.S.W., 1984. John Charadia, Teacher, a former student of mine at Good Samaritan Teacher's College, Glebe, Sydney.

[3] The ideas from this creative teaching experience were then related to my students at Catholic College of Education, Castle Hill, Sydney, for their implementation in the theory and practise of creativity in dance.

The children needed to move well. To discover the movement of the instrument—the human body. To extend the capacity for movement and the possibilities. Through the introduction of physical skills, each child could improve their flexibility, co-ordination, balance, strength, agility; the physical welfare expanded. Elementary modern dance movements were introduced, enriching the movement vocabulary.

Movement ideas for expression and creative experiences were preceded by improvisation, imaginatively exploring qualities, images, themes; the spatial factor, dynamics and contrasts in movement and accompanying sounds and music.

Working independently and in relationships with others, the class investigated and manipulated ways of moving, creating a sense of communal power. Each child became aware of his or her dance potential and emerging creative expressions, responding through awareness to the differences of others.

The perception of space changed; we welcomed moving and dancing in the open air (grass area of the playground); one could teach the movements of travelling across the space; the walks, runs, leaps, falls; in the classroom-workshop the movements were creative, expressive of individual development through dance; movements became curves, bends, extensions, twists, swings, changes of weight, shapes of body design.

Beginning as a creative exercise, the "Wasteland" re-titled Trash, developed into a finished product; a dance composition; the emphasis was on the standard of skills, movement sequences, form, interpretation of the idea, musical response, expressed through the experience of dancing and performing.[1]

There was always "something to dance about";[2]

a child stretching   another cross-legged bending the body   it snaps shut like a pen-knife   the classroom becomes a dance   the barefoot   the leaping that never stops hurtling   disappearing   breakthrough the paper cut-outs   fractions trace the number two with the pointed foot   the lazy meandering of fish   sharp edges float on the chairs   watch the colour circles vermilion a treasure hunt   side fall   scraping fingers   follow an unbroken line   germs raging bins   short life of the male mosquito   a Spanish dance rhythm   examine a blade of grass   living organisms   three variations of a puzzle see-saw fall out zig zag.

Most of the children were surprised at the physical demands of the movement, but remained alert and sensitive to the expression of ideas. Imaginative movement led some of the class into satisfying creative solutions of increasing expressiveness. Reactions to certain of the activities suggested the need for more confidence and movement resources. Yet every child is different and I discovered a few boys and girls capable of working on their own, initiating movement and organising their ideas creatively to find the very best means of personal expression; to perceive in a new way.

The recognition given by the Principal, Michael Weir, assisted in establishing the place of dance and the arts in the school, where every child could participate in an expressive arts programme. Designed and constructed by John Charadia, parents

[1] This was performed in Liverpool, Sydney, as part of the Dance Festival 1984. Title—"Wasteland", Music: Abyssales—Espaces Dynamiques—Francisco Semprun et Michael Christodoulides. Unidisc—France UD 30 1309.
[2] Doris Humphrey.

and children, The Arts Studio, Workshop and Sculpture Garden, became the centre of their aesthetic contribution to the creative needs of the school.

TRASH

We wanted to experience the sensations of dirt and decay against the innocence of purity—the ugliness of life in a world smeared by pollution—of men and women cleaning and sweeping and the presence of the stream with fluid movement, spreading, flowing, re-newing.

The waste paper buckets and bins were carried into the room—one by one we pulled out the contents—stupefying odours overcame us, slime, squalor, flyblown litter, rotting putrescence impregnated the room. The odour of impurity was pervasive. Scraps of food, stained papers, sticky sediment from cans; the overpowering malodours contaminated our environment. like scavengers we grovelled and crawled through the mess—crumpled, stained.

The experience among the waste matter and the festering impure air was further exacerbated by the dumping of more rubbish by the polluters, until we were wading in it; some were sinking into the drebris; they had become germs!

The class gave expression to their unpleasant situation and sensations, by appropriate sounds and accompanying gestures; growls, coughs, sneezes; the sound explosions were messages of their reactions.

The germs, true to their character and nature, dispersed and scattered the refuse, opposing and thwarting the efforts of the cleaners.

They would creep or crawl behind a mound of trash and litter it on the floor; slouching they would drag the scraps and rags in all directions. One was reminded of the legend of Sisyphus, who, without respite rolled his rock up a steep cliff; or the Danaids condemned eternally to fill a bottomless barrel.

During the following weeks we developed this spontaneous experience into a finished composition with essentials of body movement, shape and form; interaction and dynamics of the class groups, exits and entrances, accompaniment, costumes, colours, props.

The class had the realistic experience, as a preparation for the composition. There was also the imaginative aspect and the feeling of the unbelievable.

We took as a starting point for the theme on pollution, this impression in verse of a waste-land.

> Rainbow-coloured water and rank grass stretched for as far as one could see;
> the great chimney of the brick works dominated the hills;
> Dirty black smoke puffed out discolouring the sky;
> Water, river beds and vegetation were rimmed and coated with emerald
> smelly slime;
> Rusty iron and steel frames, tin cans, broken glass, beer bottles,
> Engulfed the marshlands.
> Here man's refuse has taken over![1]

The germs are hidden curled up in the rubbish bins. There is no movement. Stealthily, fingers appear or a hand lifts or pushes up a lid. Slow, unhurried, hesi-

[1] "The Wasteland". Mark Chaplin. *Poetry Plus, book three.* Schofield and Sims Ltd, Huddersfield, England, 1983.

Trash, "Germs"
Photograph: Ken Wilde

tant, tentative. Little by little the bins opened, lids rolled on to the floor; a leg, a head, a foot is visible; there is tension in the bodies as they twist. The expression, furtive, inward. The verminous creatures want to escape and the impact is diverse and strange.

These receptacles were placed on the floor standing upright or on their side; they covered a student's head and shoulders; some of the children were curled up in boxes or lying in plastic garbage bags.

The focus is on the movement breaking through at random and at irregular intervals. At first there is restraint. Hemmed in by the lack of space, shoulders, elbows, wrists rotate in or outward; the trunk twists; the children rear up, pushing away from their cage, they extend an arm upward or a leg is curled over the edge. They increase the force of their movement until they are standing. With strong, hard pushes these twisted shapes throw themselves forward, side or backwards over the edge of the opening of their container. Their bodies are bent, hanging downwards, almost free. The germs become exultant—the movement pattern has been circuitous.

"Here man's refuse has taken over!"

The group of "cleaners" advance with strong sharp high leg extensions towards the "germ" figures. There is a short battle, "Vermin versus Cleaners"—these "freedom from dirt" supporters confront the defiant germs and a vigorous struggle follows. The "germs" are pulled with one hand or both hands out of the bins; they hold on to the rims: they resist and are shaken out; writhing, slithering, wriggling, onto the floor. Picking up the lids the "cleaners" jump over the germs, swinging and circling the round shapes.

The combatants meet and are locked in a struggle. Each pair (germ and cleaner) grasp the lid (shield); they twist in a figure of eight, up and down; lurch in a zig-zag pattern, breakaway, attempting to change direction and free themselves. One last offensive by the attacking cleaners. Quick dodging movements forward, backward or side and they surround the enemy, overpowering the germs who fall to the floor with sharp, sudden movements. The bins are overturned, all germs are thrown off their balance and rolled across the floor and out of the space.

One by one the victorious 'cleaners', holding the bins above their heads, run, leap, skip, jump off.

We were now ready to work on the second part of this theme. A small group of children had identified and associated themselves with 'the stream'. Should we splash water around the room, or sprinkle it drop by drop—perhaps 'wash' in large scrubbing movements?

Instead of this functionalism and realism we devised a pattern of lyrical movements—a new movement image, to change the mood from ugliness to beauty—moving in unison and as a chorus; a stream of continuous movement.

"The Stream"
Photograph: Ken Wilde

Changes of weight, forward and back, side to side, upwards and downwards, met the sound of the words, "splashing in" and "splashing out"—this depicted the water parting and flowing in again.

After the side falls to the floor, the successive rising and falling of the body through the breath, changed the previous restless scene into the fresh, moving, airy motions of water. The body and parts of the body rippled and undulated—the pattern of movement changed as figures ascended and descended—they could have been drops of rain; a free flow of movement. The children described a visible curving pathway in the space.

"Wash in!" "Wash out!" Swinging arms, legs and bodies, the group were propelled by the momentum of the arc and energy of the swings across the space to a crescendo, catching the organic rhythm of flow, ebb, flow.

The stream of movement does not stop. It continues the spirit of innocence and imagination in the child and nature—the spirit—harmony. The group follow as one; the centres of the circles shift into the curve of the arm; focus changes into the cupped hand; the contours of the moving shapes wind slowly in a circular form to the floor; from up to down; the hands open slowly and release the energy—Ripplings, Murmurings, Echoes.

In contrast to this composition, the germs in Trash assumed another shape . . . they were the substance of abstract movement, achieving a different visual and kinetic interest.[1]

The young dancers were completely encased in large plastic bags (small holes to breathe through). They were to find a way of moving within that shape, of exploring ways of escaping, freeing themselves from the bags.

The space was filled with small and large irregular shapes. Lying on the floor, the figures shifted within the restrictive environment. They have lost their human image! With knees bent they crouched and shuffled, the body held in a bent position, or twisted into a spiral. One could see the movement starting in the body and flowing out to the extremities in long linear designs. The bag became a skin which reflected the contrasting activity of the movement exploration.

The dynamic tensions and the inherent energy in each plastic unit increased. Standing, sitting or lying, shapes rolled, curled, curved, twisted, spiralled; shapes changed, depending on where the weight was placed; shapes opened, closed; rocked from side to side; forwards and backwards; in proximity or placed far apart from each other, changing the level from low to high; box; corkscrew; space structure.

The impetus of the germ shapes to free themselves began firstly through the movement of fingers, elbows, foot, hand, head and knee; punching, thrusting, tearing, poking, clawing, in efforts that ranged from tentative to aggressive; wriggling, stretching, creeping, or exploding into sudden movements, freeing themselves in whatever way they wished.

Was it dark in there?

How much movement could you make?

How did you feel?

---

[1]"Variations on the theme of pollution were created and performed for The World Council for the Gifted and Talented." Hamburg 1986 with dancers from Edelgard Speckmann School of dance; Pirmin Trecu dance group, Porto 1986.

A poem about pollution was read by one of the dancers. The group responded after hearing it in their own language of German or Portuguese, thus adding extra expression to the idea.

COLLAGE COROLLARY

You can become your own re-cycling source. We opened my bags of "bits and pieces"—throw-aways to some; but to the class they were the means towards a creative experience.

The reaction was like the rush for bargains at Sale Time. There was a spontaneous response from the children, whose animated comments and actions reflected an appeal not only to their sense of enjoyment, but for a useful, aesthetic purpose.

What kind of material excites us? Let us recognise the imaginative qualities of the "found materials",[1] no longer discarded as rubbish, and relate them to movement, transforming them in a new way. The choice is your own. Create a visual image in motion.

> In this agglomeration of tantalising fragments were faded flowers, bold coloured beads, raucous plastics, melting lip salve, daring and dangerous fringes, nostalgic photographs, broken kites, flags, a playing card. Stiff, soft, shiny, stunning surfaces. Buttons, marbles, pine cones, a dance shoe, mouth organ, five feathers, pungent perfumes. Stretched, silent whispering alive stuff. Three hard-hearted sequins, fake jewellery in exotic settings, the fire of opals, the brazen lights of the diamond and the dreamy pearl; blurred spectacles; threads like icicles.

You can become a collage; try new and different ways of evoking the potential of these things; how do you perceive them—how do you relate them to movement?

Some of you will like the same qualities and textures; others will choose different colours and shapes; are you able to see a relationship in the fragments?

"Simplify or exaggerate; dawdle, sleepwalk, stiltwalk, fox-trot, unlock your dreams, memories, uncertainties. Human shape, supernatural, natural. Sad or comical games; swirling, witty, enveloping, pliable, airy. Follow the solitary bird flying in the night sky."

Look into the elements of these objects, find their characteristics.

Paste, daub, sew, hang, paint, design and arrange your collage to suit a part of the environment—to suit you—what you want to show—to be—to say—your collage needs to move—find a movement combination that will characterise your own creation. Bring out what is inside you. No set ideas; express your uncertainties; you are free to choose, to recognise, assemble and transform the materials into your own expression in movement.

The class was divided into groups; some chose to work with a partner; a few preferred to create on their own.

As this process materialized, some of the children discovered the movement patterns and qualities spontaneously and rapidly, retaining ideas from their own experience, skills and movement abilities; other children worked very slowly, need-

---

[1] "Found materials", an experimental topic in dance and the related arts. New York University, U.S.A., 1960. Professor Chandler Montgomery.

ing assistance to translate their perception into a creative unit. Single solutions were found by a few of the class who responded to a simple basis for movement; two contrasting qualities combined with a shape (hard-soft; round-straight line). The approach by one group to the sparkling lights of the gem-stones, was through syncopated responses; the impact of sharp jumps accented upwards, against the regular beat of a foot rhythm.

Expression of the novel trimmings—a collection of scraps of plastic materials—led to an incongruous effect—the movement was awkward, dissonant, unequal—the meaning is disturbing.

A linear design of the body became "a blade of grass".

The "hard-edged sequins" moved as dots—vibrating with a staccato rhythm. Will you give them a name?

The class constantly handled the materials in terms of shape, environment, textures, qualities, mood, for further movement possibilities, intensities, relationships and qualities, placing them in new and differing contexts with movement.

Like bold brush strokes your movement will be broad, wide extensions for strong colours; with your partner alternate, contrast, change direction; symmetrical body movement for the colour red, against asymmetrical lines for yellow; the body shape is curved deeply for purple.

Discover your resources for feathery movement; weightlessness, rising and gliding; fast light runs and jumps; fragmented movement; move the fingers, shoulders, feet, parts of the body as quickly and lightly as possible.

This was an interesting way to work responding and drawing on the qualities and characteristics and characteristics of these materials and relating them to movement in an unexpected way. The juxtaposition of "a dance shoe" and an old photograph gave these isolated objects a new meaning; linking them together, they were used by the children as an idea for a dance.

As I left the classroom workshop, John and the children were ablaze with ideas.

"Let's find and collect our own materials."

"Create a collage corner with posters, hangings, moving designs, space shapes, sequences of colour images."

A disguise or a discovery? The touchstone is the imagination.

"EAT THE RICH ..."

The swirling romantic script of the graffiti, contrasted oddly against its stark message leaping from the bare wall; threatening, provocative, pervasive.

Something to think about? Something to dance about? I suggested this notion to the class. Yes! The reaction was favourable and gleeful. We all wanted "To eat the rich for Christmas!"

The Misses and Mesdames posed; stepped lightly and began to promenade in front of the sight below—

It was like a shop window except that there was no glass—so the Posh Ladies could bend over and gaze with rapture at the shiny scuttling species on the ground.

120

Pouting Flim-Flam, St Kewpie Honore, Bébé Poupée, Fudge Frappé, and Tendu with a touch of Parisienne, extended and developed their elegant legs, re-pointed their dainty feet, arched their backs, moving back and forth with delicacy and finicality that was awesome. Heads wavered on shapely necks. Listen carefully for the rustlings of the finest silks—their mode, manners and movement captured a rich decorative image. Watch the fanciful and capricious styles of movement emphasise the "airs and graces" of these Posh Painted Ladies.

One received a different impression from the heaving crowd on the floor, moving in eccentric patterns. Figures in the shape and form of lobsters lumbered about with feverish curiosity—inelegant and uncouth they squatted low on their haunches, in deep, low bends, moving arms and legs stiffly, all movement kept as low to the floor as possible. They clambered over each other or clasped and hugged a partner, then stomped about together—gawkish.

The Posh Ones interrupted their slow and stately walking, watched these creatures, and assumed an attitude of silent affectation—elbows bent, hands turned up or dropped at the wrist.

But the lobster's excitement and hence their agility increased—they formed fours and began to execute what can only be described as a military manoeuvre.

Moving in a rigid pattern and beating a slow drumming rhythm with their feet and legs; the group became one in the Lobster Quadrille.[1] Expressions changed from one of drollery to aggression—the formalised marching ceased—and thrusting, vigor-ous, vehement efforts by the lobster horde increased as they attempted to reach up and pull down the ladies perched above them. The whole unloving, scrambling, rear-ing mass accelerated their frenzied efforts.

The entire company of the elegant ladies stood poised, balanced, antipathetic and disdainful. "Ladies who stroll on terraces adjacent to the sea; baby girls and giantesses, superb blacks in the verdigius mass, jewels upright in the rich ground of groves and little thawed gardens."[2]

The claw-like hand movements of the aggressors quickened—strong, disjointed movements of arms, legs, as they clawed their way from the floor to standing, level with their adversaries. As they attacked the Posh ones. Bébé Poupée rose up on her toes and fell forwards and downwards—she entered the writing mass stiffly—Tendu with a touch of Parisienne, Flim-Flam and the others resisted their attackers briefly and fell down in quick succession. Only Fudge Frappé recoiled; she half turned as if to run and leap away, but the most malevolent of the horde sprang up after her and grabbed her by the ankle. For one instant she seemed to be suspended in the air and then crumpled, falling face downwards into the amorphous heap.

The preparations for the banquet began. Poupée and Frappé were arranged in a pose, as the centrepiece. Flim-Flam was so flexible that she was twisted into a near impossible shape; part of the decoration. The Lobsters completed the table setting by arranging the victims side by side on the floor, then attacked the vain glorious ladies with gusto. Legs and arms were bent in various ways and directions, using cut-ting, slicing and chopping movements: . . . toes and fingers delicately separated . . . "Eat the rich for Christmas!"

[1] Alice's Adventures under Ground. Lewis Carroll. Dover Publications, New York, 1965.
[2] Illuminations. Arthur Rimbaud. New Directions Paperback, New York, 1957.

THE LAST WAVE

Can we interpret The Last Wave by Hokusai?[1] What does it reveal to us? what has it got to do with our sense of movement?

The contours were breathing, spontaneous, successive, vigorous. Some of us saw the swirling lines differently:

Snow Clouds
Fingers
A Sand Storm
Broken Wing
Great Cliff of Snow
the Engulfing Volcano
Sleep—The Scream[2]

Can we achieve a movement motif by a succession of parallel strokes of a part of our body, e.g. small parallel movements of the feet and arms—or stippled effect by staccato-like jabs—of the hand or head?

I think we could interpret this imagery through the body with quality and form by

The Last Wave
Photograph: Ken Wilde

[1] Katsushuka Hokusai—Japanese painter (1760–1842).
[2] An awakening—A Hidden Reality, Looming, Devouring, Kafkaesque-MUNCH.

using broader, heavier near-abstract shapes for more dramatic movement; increasing the dimensions of the circular group designs.

"Travel across the space vanishing at different points, time and levels. Exploit the speed of travelling through differences in shape curved or linear."

Let the group travel forward, one figure in the group moving backwards against the regular rhythm.

As you move, take the whole time to curve forwards shaping the body; will gravity succeed within this time duration to lead you to the floor?' Each one will experience their own sense of time and the sense of shape.

"Try moving with small steps and as you fall forward, resist, draw the energy inwards and pull up the body, feel the weight of the gravitational pull and the response of your body weight, shape, movement . . . pull upward, curve downward, upward. Run, back wave, finish the rippling movement on the knees; engulfing."

In pairs or in small groups evolve a movement pattern of waves, sideways, forwards, backwards with a half turn; a small forward curve, changing the body design to a slow, deep, back curve.

Let the movement flow through the shoulders, elbow, wrist, hands, arms, knee, hip, head, use the breath to motivate the undulating rhythms.

The last wave?

FIGURES OF EIGHT IN THE SPACE

"Every movement made by a human being . . . has a design in space . . ."[1]

Bodies were defined in the space by their movement designs evolving out of the lines of the figure of eight. A range of dynamics unfolded in successive body designs of eights, threes, twos and loops.

"The direction will be along the diagonal line; starting independently, you may change the movement pattern and direction in the space, after you have explored the first set of movement shapes and designs."

The class began with the forward walks. After four walking steps they describe the figure of eight with the foot and the hand.

Draw the figure three on a horizontal plane;

Make an air design with curved lines;

With a smooth movement of the arm, design a loop; let it sweep around your body.

Move across the floor; change the circular designs; a looping movement by the limbs.

Slide and push your body along the floor; draw your designs at that level with parts of your body.

Run in the pattern of a figure of eight;

Make narrow and wide designs; hold the body in a bent position;

Reverse the designs;

[1] Gertrud Bodenwieser, Modern dance technique.

Small groups move across the space in a diagonal line.

slow or fast

in running or in a triplet

jumping loops

tracing a figure of eight in the space by a running design

Quick shifting of designs of movement by individuals or contrast between any one or a number of the fifteen dancers.

Choose their own point to enter the space.

Numbers 1, 2 & 3, begin from the corner moving across the diagonal successively.

Number 4 chooses a different diagonal; slower movement, larger circles of the body or legs or arms.

Number 5 is a *still* figure in the centre, and designs her own looping movements.

Number 6 reverses the direction along the diagonal moving from the end to the starting point.

Numbers 7 & 8 run together describing circles in the space and run a figure of eight.

Numbers 9 & 10 move along the floor at a low level expanding the figure two, moving in unison.

Number 11 moves backwards along the diagonal line in small jumps and loops.

Number 12, figure of eight running, in turning or with contraction in small circles.

Numbers 13, 14 & 15 sustain a rhythmic pattern of circular lines through repetition.

In a separate space one metre square encapsulate the basic design of your movement. Reduce the size of the floor pattern and body design to minimal movement.

Run in a circle, stop, shake parts of the body. Ankles, feet, knees, pelvis, torso, elbows, shoulders, neck, head; let the limbs tremble. Sense the differences in movement as you release your muscles. Shake all parts of your body. Repeat runs, shaking, trembling. Shuffle towards the centre—bodies droop downwards.

Group Contact. Connections are made between figures—they loop, bend, curve—juxtaposition of bodies moving as a group on the diagonal line—tension and counter-tension between the figures loosen their grasp and break away from each other, running freely into the diagonal space . . . to be pulled back . . . a density of movement.

A calm beginning ending in convolutions of movement designs, progressing to a crescendo of energy; of trembling, shaking, looping, pushing and pulling; utilizing through the movement a balance between dynamic forces.[1]

★　　　★　　　★

---

[1] This movement idea was developed for The Creative Dance Theatre Group, Utah, U.S.A., Dance and The Child International Conference, London, 1988.

We have been involved throughout this book in the extraordinary process of creativity and now each one may need to search and release their own individual imagining. To find their way as choreographers or creative teachers through the labyrinth of human experience. The half-remenbered innocence; the purity of movement and its eloquent potential for those who dance ... away from stifling conformism, to a freedom of spirit and the recognition of the power of dance as an art form in our society.

Without invention nothing is well spaced, unless the mind change, unless the stars are new measured, according to their relative positions, the line will not change the necessity will not matriculate: unless there is a new mind there cannot be a new line, the old will go on repeating itself with recurring deadlines: without invention.[1]

[1] *Modernism in Literature; Bender, Armstrong, Briggum, Knobloch.* William Carlos Williams. Paterson, Book II. Holt, Rinehart and Winston, New York, 1977.

"How Can We Know the Dancer from the Dance?"

Labour is blossoming or dancing where
the body is not bruised to pleasure soul,
Nor beauty born out of its own despair,
Nor blear-eyed wisdom out of mid-night oil.
O Chestnut-Tree, great-rooted blossomer,
Are you the leaf, the blossom or the hole?
O body swayed to music, O brightening glance
How can we know the dancer from the dance?[1]

I reflected on the nature of the "perceptions, fancies, feelings, and thoughts of the poet W. B. Yeats" at a moment of human life, as he addresses himself to the question, "How can we know the dancer from the dance?"[2]

Yeats confides in us that he is seeking the ideal; a way to approach humanity and a meaning of art; resolving the conflict between the real and the unreal; translating the expression of his convictions about the world through poetry.

He searches with creative energy for the possibilities to convey his reactions and convictions to the world with passionate intensity; through his intellect, emotion, experience; drawing consolation from the idea and pursuit of the qualities of the imagination as expressed in art to satisfy the permanence or survival of individual life.

Permanence has always eluded him but he finds in the symbols of "the dancer and the dance" an indivisible oneness, a unity that he is so intent on possessing; one being; of youth and beauty, delighting in the shape and form of movement and expression; of the body in dance as a life force.

Thoughts and images of children float into his mind—the innocent bloom of youthful beauty—soon to fade—despising old age he sees his own body shape as that of a scarecrow "Old clothes upon old sticks to scare a bird".[3]

He questions, "Is not beauty bound up with the body and doomed to decay with

[1] The excerpt is from the poem in "The Tower" called "Among School Children". *The Collected Poems of W. B. Yeats, Definitive Edition*. The MacMillan Company, New York, 1958.
[2] *The Permanence of Yeats*. Edited by James Hall and Martin Steinmann. First Collier Books Edition, U.S.A., 1961.
[3] "Among School Children", from "The Tower". *The Collected Poems of W. B. Yeats. Definitive Edition*. The MacMillan Company, U.S.A., 1958.

it?"[1] Never reconciled to old age or the diminution of power, strength, beauty and youth, can Yeats take refuge in the inseparability of "the dancer and the dance"? believing in it to satisfy his deepest impulse? . . . To create poems of lasting value.

It seems that many of his immediate responses are of a physical nature, deriving a personal sensation from the dynamic element of the dance; he feels its physical necessity. His creative mind flowing through the imagination uses "words with dance";[2] references and allusions to dance are expressed in some poetic works, which he feels will reinforce and enrich his ideas.

> Birth-hour and death-hour
> OR, as great sages say,
> Men dance on deathless feet[3]

> the girl goes dancing there
> On the leaf-sown, new-mown smooth
> Grass plot of the garden;
> Escaped out of her crowd,
> OR out of her black cloud.
> Ah, dancer, ah, sweet dancer![4]

> She might, so noble from head
> To great shapely knees
> The long flowing line[5]

> That crazed girl improvising her music,
> her poetry, dancing upon the shore,
> her soul in division from itself
> climbing, falling she knew not where.[6]

> When Loie Fuller's Chines dancers unwound
> A Shining web, a floating ribbon of cloth,
> It seemed that a dragon of air
> Had fallen among dancers, had wheeled them round
> Or hurried them off on its own furious path;
> So the Platonic Year
> Whirls in the old instead;
> All men are dancers and their tread
> Goes to the barbarous clangour of a gong[7]

Dance for Yeats is divine, of inner spiritual origins; of all joy, harmony, enhancement. He emphasizes its elusive nature . . . the ephemerality.

He seeks in it vitality, energy, imaginative life, and regeneration of the spirit;

---

[1] From a critical essay by Edmund Wilson in *The Permanence of Yeats*. Edited by James Hall and Martin Steinmann. First Collier Books Edition, U.S.A., 1961.

[2] Critical Essay by New York Theatre and Drama Critic, Eric Bentley; the use of music and dance by Yeats in poetry and drama, combining dance and spoken words; he wrote "Four Plays for Dancers"; Yeats . . . a poet, playwright and man of theatre who asks of his acts—movement, dance. From *The Permanence of Yeats*. Edited by James Hall and Martin Steinmann. First Collier Books Edition, U.S.A., 1961.

[3] The lines are excerpts from a poem, Mohini Chatterjee.

[4] "Sweet Dancer".

[5] "A Thought from Propertius".

[6] "A Crazed Girl".

[7] "Nineteen Hundred and Nineteen".

indeed for Yeats the essence of the dance is in all art forms and in this way aspires to order his own existence, coming close to fulfilment; to infinity.

For man through the centuries has inherited countless movements—an expression of his life, his myths, made tangible and visible in the cosmos by rhythmic movement. Many years after the external element of the human body has vanished, he predicts that art will live on in the spirit of man.

For the "dancer and the dance" there is the archaic innocence, springing from a sphere of its own; knowing about life, feeling its meaning; distilling the fragments of life's experience through the motion of dance; the trust is in our imagination; of extending the horizons beyond old age, loss of youth, beauty, the mortal self, to the far-reaching spirit of immortality.

Perhaps it was the kinship which Yeats felt for the dance which led him unknowingly to follow a vision of dance as expressed by Martha Graham.

"The reality of the dance is its Truth to our inner life."

Selected Reading

Arts & Ideas (6th Edition), William Fleming. Holt, Rinehart and Winston, New York, 1980.

The Uses of Enchantment. Bruno Bettelheim. Penguin Books, England, 1976.

The Strength to Dream. Colin Wilson. Abacus, London, reprint 1982.

Towards a Poor Theatre. Jerzys Grotowski. A Clarion book published by Simon and Schuster, New York, 1968.

Gateway to the Dance. Ruby Ginner. Newman Neame Limited, Great Britain, 1960.

Changes: Notes on Choreography. Merce Cunningham. Something Else Press Inc., New York, 1968.

The Language of Dance. Mary Wigman. Macdonald & Evans Ltd., London, 1966.

Gordon Craig on Movement and Dance. Edited, and with an Introduction by Arnold Rood. Dance Books, London, 1977.

Experimental Theatre. James Roose. Evans Studio Vista, London, 1979.

Man Ray. The Rigour of Imagination. Arturo Schwarz. Thames and Hudson Ltd, London, 1977.

Paul Klee on Modern Art. Faber & Faber Limited, London, 1966.

The Dramatic Imagination (13th Printing). Robert Edmond Jones. Theatre Arts Books, 1980.

Music and Dance. Editor D. Tunley. Department of Music, The University of Western Australia, Perth, 1982.

The Creative Process. Edited by Brewster Ghiselin. A Mentor book, University of California Press, 1955.

The Poetic Image. C. Day Lewis. Jonathan Cape, Great Britain, 1947.

Imagination. Mary Warnock. Faber and Faber, London, 1976.

Creativity Across the Curriculum. Millicent Poole. George Allen & Unwin Pty Ltd, Australia, 1980.

The Dynamics of Creation. Anthony Storr. Pelican Books, England, 1976.

Creativity, The Magic Synthesis. Silvano Arieti. Basic Books Inc. Publishers, New York, 1976.

The Empty Space. Peter Brook. Atheneum, New York, 1981.